LIGUORI CHRISTIAN INITIATIC

Journey of Faith

FOR TEENS

CATECHUMENATE LEADER GUIDE

Liguori PUBLICATIONS

A Redemptorist Ministry

Journey of Faith for Teens Catechumenate Leader Guide (827143)

Imprimi Potest: Stephen T. Rehrauer, CSsR, Provincial, Denver Province, the Redemptorists

Imprimatur: "In accordance with CIC 827, permission to publish has been granted on July 26, 2016, the Rev. Msgr. Mark S. Rivituso, Vicar General, Archdiocese of St. Louis. Permission to publish is an indication that nothing contrary to Church teaching is contained in this work. It does not imply any endorsement of the opinions expressed in the publication; nor is any liability assumed by this permission."

Text: Adapted from *Journey of Faith for Adults* © 2000 Liguori Publications.
Editor of 2016 edition: Theresa Nienaber. Design: Lorena Mitre Jimenez. Images: Shutterstock.

Printed in the United States of America
20 19 18 17 16 / 5 4 3 2 1
Third Edition

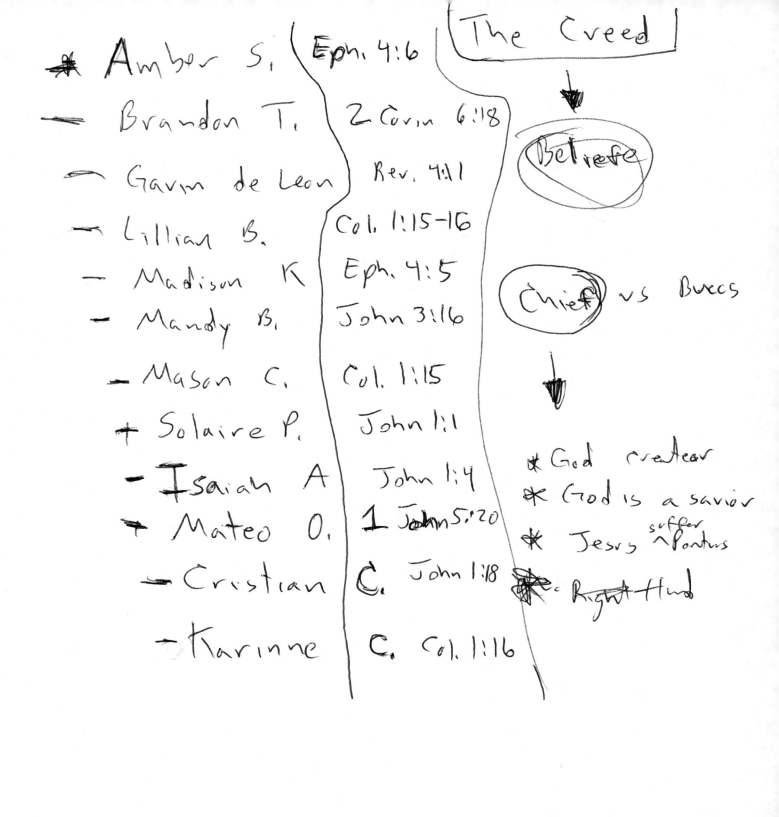

* Amber S. (Eph. 4:6
- Brandon T. 2 Corin 6:18
- Garin de Leon Rev. 4:11
- Lillian B. Col. 1:15-16
- Madison K Eph. 4:5
- Mandy B. John 3:16
- Mason C. Col. 1:15
+ Solaire P. John 1:1
- Isaiah A John 1:4
+ Mateo O. 1 John 5:20
- Cristian C. John 1:18
- Karinne C. Col. 1:16

The Creed

Believe

Chief vs Buccs

* God creator
* God is a savior
* Jesus suffer Pontus
* Right Hand

Contents

The Catechumenate: A Period and A Process

Since the early Church, generally "the catechumenate" referred to the entire process of Christian conversion and initiation. It spanned multiple years and involved formal instruction, acts of penitence, and public rites that confirmed the community's approval as well as the catechumen's changed status.

Today, the term *catechumenate*, and *catechumen* in some respects, refers to a specific stage within the typical RCIA process. The rite of acceptance has been called a "first step," even though most participants take part in a period of inquiry as well as unknown years of personal discernment before contacting a Catholic parish (*RCIA* 42). While the rite of election technically "closes the period of the catechumenate proper," catechumens (then the *elect*) and candidates continue to meet for months and have not yet been fully initiated (*RCIA* 118; see also *National Statutes for the Catechumenate*, 6).

The period of the catechumenate remains at the heart of the RCIA process. Team members, catechists, and participants should take advantage of all its benefits and allow it to progress naturally. It may be best to extend the length of this period rather than rushing through or shortchanging the participant's needs and experiences, especially when an inquirer enters the process later than others, Lent arrives early, or there are exceptional circumstances.

While the catechumenate is distinctly reserved for more formal instruction and presentation of essential doctrine, it is also a time for participants to practice and apply their faith. The Church identifies four goals for the catechumenate (*RCIA* 75). During this period, participants will:

1. receive a "suitable catechesis…planned to be gradual and complete in its coverage….This catechesis leads the catechumens not only to an appropriate acquaintance with dogmas and precepts but also to a profound sense of the mystery of salvation…" (see also Decree on the Missionary Activity of the Church [*Ad Gentes*], 14, from the Second Vatican Council).

2. "become familiar with the Christian way of life…, learn to turn more readily to God in prayer, … and to practice love of neighbor, even at the cost of self-renunciation."

3. participate in "suitable liturgical rites, which purify the catechumens little by little and strengthen them with God's blessing….

At Mass they may also take part with the faithful in the Liturgy of the Word, thus better preparing themselves for their eventual participation in the liturgy of the Eucharist."

4. "learn how to work actively with others to spread the Gospel and build up the Church.…"

Throughout the catechumenate, catechumens and candidates will undergo "a progressive change of outlook and morals" (*AG* 13). RCIA leaders and sponsors can be catalysts for this spiritual transformation by providing opportunities for reflection, interaction with the community, and by supporting their study with clear and accurate information. Many features of the *Journey of Faith* program and materials assist you in achieving those goals.

Prior to the rite of election, leaders, sponsors, and participants themselves should observe an increase in the participant's understanding and ownership of his or her Catholic Christian faith. The signing of names into the *Book of the Elect* signifies the fuller "yes" to Christ and Church that began in his or her heart at the rite of acceptance.

Rites Belonging to the Catechumenate

Celebrations of the Word of God
The catechumenate, indeed the entire RCIA process, is connected intrinsically to the liturgical year. The Church's recommendation that it last at least one year is to ensure that catechumens experience the fullness of the paschal mystery as reflected in the liturgy.

Many RCIA groups attend the Sunday Liturgy of the Word together. Others meet during the week to proclaim and reflect on the upcoming readings. You may combine these celebrations with the catechetical sessions or keep them separate. However you structure your RCIA process, maintaining a connection to the seasons of the Church year and regularly, prayerfully breaking open the Scriptures are vitally important. *The Word Into Life*—available in three volumes for Sunday cycles A, B, and C—provides the full text of the readings along with commentaries and questions for an RCIA audience.

Model for a Celebration of the Word of God

1. *Song.* The celebration opens with an appropriate hymn or chant.

2. *Readings and Responsorial Psalm.* A baptized member, ideally a trained lector, proclaims a reading or two from Scripture. As in Mass, the first or Old Testament readings are followed by a psalm, either sung or in a call-and-response format.

3. *Lesson.* The RCIA director, pastor, or another trained catechist briefly explains and applies the readings.

4. *Concluding Rites.* The celebration closes with a prayer or one or more of the optional rites below (*RCIA* 85–89).

Optional Rites

Catechumens and candidates can be nourished by other liturgical rites during this period. The Church offers texts and guidelines for minor exorcisms (petitions for strength in the challenges of faith and struggle against temptation), blessings, and anointings, which may occur on their own or conclude a celebration of the word (*RCIA* 90–103). Speak to your priest or deacon about when and how these might benefit your particular group.

Also, you will need to determine what rites are appropriate for the period of enlightenment and how they will fit into the weeks leading up to the Easter Vigil. The presentations of the Creed and the Lord's Prayer can be moved to late in the catechumenate if necessary, but the priest, deacon, or DRE should ensure that the catechumens are ready beforehand. If the rites of election and/or calling are celebrated by the bishop elsewhere in the diocese, both the parish and participants will benefit from the *rite of sending.* In this rite, the local pastor and community preliminarily approve and celebrate the participants' readiness (see *RCIA* 106–17, 434–45, 530–46). It demonstrates their present, though distant, love and support and strengthens the catechumens and candidates for their return and entrance into the Lenten season.

The Rite of Election

The rite of election is a major milestone in the catechumens' RCIA journey. Usually occurring on the first Sunday of Lent, catechumens' publicly pledge their fidelity to the Church and sign the *Book of the Elect.* Baptized candidates participate in the *rite of calling the candidates to continuing conversion* or in a combined rite. These rites are similar, but do not include any signing.

The *Journey of Faith* program provides a basic outline to the rite of election in lesson C1: *The RCIA Process and Rites* and spiritual preparation through Scripture and reflection in lesson E1 *Election: Saying Yes to Jesus.*

"Before the rite of election the bishop, priests, deacons, catechists, godparents, and the entire community [should] arrive at a judgment about the catechumens' state of formation and progress" (*RCIA* 121). This doesn't mean an interview or exam is needed; however, pastors who have not attended the RCIA sessions may want to briefly speak to you about the group.

This is a good time to gather the team members' and sponsors' feedback and experiences with the catechumens. Recording and sharing particularly meaningful input or stories can serve as a testimony to the individual's faith as well as to the power of the Spirit working in and through your parish RCIA.

The bishop ordinarily admits catechumens and candidates to their respective rites and presides at the ceremony. Whether or not the rite of election is celebrated in your parish, encourage all team members, sponsors, and close family and friends to attend. Prepare the catechumens by reviewing the steps or rehearsing the responses ahead of time. The steps of the rite are listed below.

1. The rite, held within a Mass, begins with the Liturgy of the Word.

2. After the homily, the celebrant calls the catechumens forward by name, along with their godparents.

3. He addresses the assembly and asks the godparents if these men and women are "worthy to be admitted" (*RCIA* 131). He asks if they have "sufficiently prepared…faithfully listened to God's word… [and] responded." The godparents answer, "They have."

4. He asks the catechumens if they wish to enter the Church. They answer, "We do."

5. After their names are signed in the *Book of the Elect,* the celebrant declares that they are members of the elect. He exhorts them to remain faithful and "to reach the fullness of truth" and their godparents to continue their "loving care and example" (*RCIA* 133).

6. The community offers intercessions for the elect.

7. The celebrant prays over the elect and dismisses them before continuing with the Liturgy of the Eucharist.

Sponsors and Godparents: Knowing and Making the Difference

The work of the parish (RCIA) sponsor usually begins during the period of inquiry and continues through the catechumenate. Since the official role ends with the beginning of Lent, the catechumen will choose a *godparent* for baptism. The godparent might be from outside the parish. He or she is ideally someone who has been and will continue to be a Christian model and support for the catechumen through life. It's the godparent's role to present the catechumen at the rite of election and to accompany him or her through the final, intense preparation for initiation. The godparent will also stand with the elect at the celebration of the sacraments and help with his or her continuing Christian formation after Easter. While many parish sponsors serve as godparents, or confirmation sponsors if their candidates are already baptized, all sponsors can continue to offer prayer and support throughout the initiation process and beyond.

Like the sponsor, a godparent must be an active Catholic. Anyone with a preexisting acquaintance is favorable, but the godparent probably should not be a close relative. Godparents should be able to judge the catechumen's progress and faith objectively and challenge him or her in Christian living. This responsibility may interfere with the personal support that naturally comes from family, and not all loved ones feel qualified or prepared. Candidates with eligible baptismal godparents may call on them to be confirmation sponsors. Once a godparent is chosen and approved, invite him or her to the weekly sessions and any preparations for the rites.

Both sponsors and godparents are companions who travel with their participant, represent the Catholic Church, and witness to his or her deepening relationship with Christ. Not everyone travels the same distance or at the same pace, but all learn from each other along the way. The personal connections made through these relationships form and unite the parish and larger Christian community. Encourage them to enjoy the journey.

Effective Catechesis during the Catechumenate

The goal of catechesis in the RCIA is conversion rather than academic or religious mastery. It should be clear, direct, and presented at the participants' level. It must be accurate and promote understanding and acceptance. It must touch their hearts and shine the light of faith on their lives. It must connect to their personal experiences or risk being discarded as irrelevant.

The catechetical model or process of faith formation generally involves three things:

1. *Life experience.*

2. *Message or doctrine.*

3. *Response.*

Personal witness is important in most, if not all, groups that discuss topics of faith, especially the RCIA. As catechists, sponsors, and participants share their stories, they begin to shape a small faith community. They better understand each other's questions, support the personal journeys of others, and reflect on their own.

The sacraments are central to the Christian life and therefore to the *Journey of Faith* catechumenate sessions as well. The images and symbols associated with each sacrament convey scriptural and theological meaning and directly relate to what we do as Catholics. Knowing this is essential to understanding and accepting our faith and will deepen the sacramental and liturgical experiences of all.

The best RCIA program goes beyond the weekly sessions to include private prayer; spiritual reading or study; and acts of charity, justice, or mercy. The process increasingly involves the community of faith, family, and others. As you approach the Easter Vigil, seek out ways in which catechumens and candidates can apply the topics and concepts and witness to their growing faith in both word and action.

Practical Suggestions

- Once participants begin attending Mass or celebrating the word, establish signals and routines that reinforce religious devotion. Sponsors can assist you in modeling proper behaviors until participants have internalized them.

- Make the best use of your materials and resources. Learn the strengths and weaknesses of various formats, media, and types of presentations. Study the *Journey of Faith* content for prayer and activity suggestions. Know when and how to supplement lesson topics, both to individuals and to all participants.

- Learn your catechumens' and candidates' needs and preferences. Continue to leave time for questions and concerns. Adjust the environment and sessions to engage many types of learners and increase understanding. Simple things like prayers, decorations, and refreshments can add interest and a personal touch.

- Connect with spiritual directors in your area. Encourage their services for all participants and make them readily available.

- When presenting the sacraments, allow catechumens to explore and interact with them. Share photos and videos of recent ceremonies. Invite sponsors, clergy, and others to describe their experiences. Compare them to traditions and symbols in other cultures.

- Bring salvation and Church history to life. Show a scene from a modern rendition of an event in the Bible or the life of a saint. Read or distribute short excerpts from magisterial documents. Share an article, press release, or stream a video from a Catholic news source on a current event or relevant topic.

Integrating the Parish Community

For many in the parish, the rites of acceptance and welcoming are a first glimpse into the RCIA process and at the new participants. This increased visibility is a prime opportunity to begin or renew the community's involvement. As the RCIA team and participants develop a rapport and feel more comfortable with the process, continue to seek out ways in which they can interact with their family in faith.

- Ensure that the pastor formally dismisses the RCIA group during Mass from the rite of acceptance until the Easter Vigil. Publicly acknowledging the catechumens' and candidates' presence affirms their dedication and heightens the community's awareness of and appreciation for this ministry. The priest's blessing also strengthens their faith and study.

- During Advent, attend a seasonal prayer service, devotion, or adoration together to expose participants to Catholic traditions.

- Remind parishioners to pray for the catechumens and candidates, to introduce themselves before or after Mass, and to share their faith with others.

- Invite parishioners to attend the weekly sessions and RCIA rites. This better reflects the communal nature of the process and demonstrates the Church's ongoing support.

- Involve team members, sponsors, and ministry members in acquiring supplies, religious objects, and audio and visual aides. Often people have these things already, eliminating the need for a purchase.

- Invite parish ministers and volunteers to speak to the participants, especially if their role or group hasn't been introduced:

  ○ The liturgy committee, music director, sacristans, or wedding coordinator might share how they prepare for Mass, sacraments, and funerals.

  ○ A Bible-study or youth group might provide some information or resources on key Bible passages or events in Church history.

  ○ The pro-life team or St. Vincent de Paul Society might give examples of how they are defending human dignity and life and working for justice in the local community. They could also invite participants to contribute or volunteer.

C1: The RCIA Process and Rites

Catechism: 1229–1233, 1247–1249

Objectives

- Describe the various rites in the RCIA and recognize where they're located in the process.
- Distinguish between the rites for catechumens and those for baptized candidates.
- Distinguish between the required (proper) and optional rites.
- Conclude that each rite results in a greater commitment to and unity with the greater Church.

Leader Meditation

John 1:35–42

Like the prophets before him, John the Baptist pointed the way to God and prepared individuals to hear and respond to the invitation to come and follow. While paths and intentions vary from person to person, we can shine light on Christ, the one who reveals who we are and gathers and unites us in his name.

Leader Preparation

- Read the lesson, this lesson plan, the Scripture passage, and *Catechism* sections.
- Review lesson Q1, its lesson plan, and this guide's front sections on the periods and rites of RCIA.
- If you haven't already, determine each participant's sacramental status and formation level. Be prepared to explain the differences as they relate to the process; refer to this guide, parish or diocesan policies, or the *rites* themselves.
- Gather any necessary instructions on your parish's rites of acceptance and welcoming, photos and videos of past RCIA rites, and/or schedule a former RCIA participant or parish pastor to share their experiences of the season.
- Be familiar with the following vocabulary terms: rite of acceptance, candidate, rite of welcoming, rite of election, elect, presentation of the Creed, presentation of the Lord's Prayer, neophyte. Definitions are provided in this guide's glossary.

Welcome

Greet participants as they arrive. Check for supplies and immediate needs. Solicit questions or comments about the previous session and/or share new information and findings. Begin promptly.

Opening Scripture

John 1:35–42

Ask one of the participants to light the candle and read the passage aloud. Remind them that this is an account of Jesus' calling his first disciples, and that Jesus is calling each of us, too. Allow for a moment of silence, then welcome any reactions. Before beginning your discussion of the lesson handout, ask participants: **What can the Catholic Church teach you? What have you found in Jesus?**

> The mystery of Christ is so unfathomably rich that it cannot be exhausted by its expression in any single liturgical tradition. The history of the blossoming and development of these rites witnesses to a remarkable complementarity.
>
> *CCC 1201*

Journey of Faith

C1

In Short:

- The RCIA includes multiple rites.
- Rites are different for catechumens and candidates.
- Some rites are required, others optional.

The RCIA Process and Rites

At some point in your life, something or someone affected your outlook on faith. Realizing your need for God may have been a gradual thing. It may have snuck up on you. But no matter how it happened, it left you changed.

Maybe that was the time you started going to your local parish. Or maybe that's where you first met God. Maybe you were invited by friends who made you feel at home. You may have been changed by a youth group that made you feel like you were part of something, that you could help others. Or maybe it was being part of a family reconnecting with the Church that got you thinking about your own beliefs.

Wherever you started, it has brought you here—to the RCIA. Now what?

- *Take time to reflect on whatever it was that got you here. What are your expectations as you move forward with the RCIA?*
- *What do you hope to get out of being a Catholic? To give to your faith?*

?

Joining the Catechumenate

If You're Unbaptized: You may already know this is the route for you. This is how unbaptized adults learn about the Catholic faith and prepare for full initiation. During the **rite of acceptance**, a ritual that makes you part of the catechumenate, you tell the community you want to follow the gospel as a member of the Church. Then your sponsor talks about your ongoing conversion. But this isn't the end. Your faith will continue to evolve through witness, word, and prayer. This path leads to the sacraments of initiation.

If You're Already Baptized: Maybe you were already baptized in another Christian church. If that's the case, you'll enter the process as a **candidate** through the **rite of welcoming**. You'll spend time talking and learning about your faith with others, then come into full communion with the Church by making a profession of faith and receiving the sacraments of confirmation and Eucharist.

You may also enjoy some optional rites, such as: celebrations of the word of God, blessings, anointing, and sending. These will be explained in more detail in later lessons.

- *Which rite will you be participating in?*

?

After Catechumenate

Purification and Enlightenment
(Lent) Once you've figured out if you're ready for this next step, you'll go through the **rite of election**. Now you are accepted to receive the

CCC 1229–1233, 1247–1249

Joining the Catechumenate

- Ask participants how many are unbaptized or baptized. Emphasize that the separate rites aren't to exclude but to eventually unite everyone in the same sacraments.

- While baptism will be discussed in more detail in lesson *C3*, if participants have questions about why those baptized in another faith tradition do not have to be rebaptized in the Catholic Church, you can refer them to the section of the Catechism on baptism which starts at CCC 1213. You can also cite *Ephesians 4:5*, which states that there is "one Lord, one faith, one baptism."

Purification and Enlightenment

- After reading "Purification and Enlightenment" ask participants to share their response to the reflection question.

As participants reflect on the answer to this question, remind them they can find inspiration and help in the saints, prayers, or inspirational books as well as living Catholics.

The RCIA Process and Rites

- Read the introductory text together. Let participants respond to reflection questions on their own, and then ask volunteers to share their responses with the group.

- *What are your expectations as you move forward with RCIA?*
  As participants share their responses, emphasize that they'll get from the RCIA what they put into it—just like with their faith. If you went through the RCIA, share how your expectations changed over time. If you're having visitors, share personal testimony in your class and consider having them introduce themselves by sharing their own response to this question.

- *What do you hope to get out of being Catholic? To give to your faith?*
  If you have any personal experience to share about how your attitude toward your faith changed what you were able to take away from it, share that now or have a visitor to your class share his or her response.

Mystagogy

- Read "Mystagogy." Discuss why it's important that the process of conversion be ongoing. Asks participants how they see their new faith becoming a part of their everyday lives.

The RCIA Rites, Close Up

- Go through each stage of the rites of acceptance and welcoming. Ask participants if they have any questions. Do the same for the other rites.

- If you have the time and opportunity, you may want to give time after each rite to allow your guest speakers to share personal testimony that puts the rite into a real-life context.

- Allot time for a personal testimony from a former RCIA participant (commonly an existing team member or sponsor). Consider inviting the pastor to share his experience and perspective as a celebrating minister. (Sharing personal experiences will help balance the reality of the rites with the technical, sometimes confusing, language used to explain them.)

sacraments of initiation. If you're already baptized, it's your decision to choose the Catholic Church that's accepted. You're now one of the **elect**. Your journey continues with more conversation and prayer throughout Lent.

- Who or what is helping you most in your journey? What does that witness mean to you?

Sacraments of Initiation

A lot of RCIA alums say this is the most overwhelming part of the experience: being baptized, confirmed, and receiving the Eucharist for the first time. At the Easter Vigil, you become a Catholic surrounded by RCIA team members, your sponsor or godparents, family, friends, and all those attending. You're now considered a neophyte. A **neophyte** is someone who is "newly planted" in the faith and has just entered into the life of the Church.

Mystagogy

After receiving the sacraments, you'll continue to talk about your faith for the rest of the Easter season, until Pentecost. This means sharing in the mysteries of the gospel and sacraments with others in your church. Even if you already feel comfortable in this community, these conversations will help you feel even more at home. Attending Mass and receiving the Eucharist are now part of your routine. Seeking to serve also pushes you into an active faith life.

"Whoever serves me must follow me, and where I am, there also will my servant be."

John 12:26

The RCIA Rites, Close Up

These rites happen at the beginning of Mass or after the homily. You'll respond to prayers spoken by the celebrating priest as you stand near the altar with your sponsor and the other RCIA candidates. Your parish may give you more specific instructions about how these rites are celebrated. You might even rehearse ahead of time.

Rite of Acceptance or Welcoming

For this rite, you are accepted into the Order of Catechumens if you are unbaptized, or welcomed into the Catholic Church if you've been previously baptized. You will now have a sponsor, and he or she will stand with you at the doors of the church to show you your movement into the community. Here's what you can expect:

1. The priest introduces each catechumen or candidate by name and asks, "What do you ask of the Church?" You respond, "Faith." You desire to live, learn, and love with the community.

2. The priest marks the sign of the cross on your forehead, a symbol of the love and strength of Jesus Christ that is with you on this journey.

3. You are invited to enter the church and join in the Liturgy of the Word. After hearing readings from the Bible, you may be called forward and given a copy of the *Book of the Gospels* or a cross. The community prays for you and sends you out to pray and think about the readings.

Rite of Election

Usually, this rite is celebrated by the bishop on the first Sunday of Lent. Here's what you can expect:

1. Your godparents will go with you to the cathedral and testify that you are ready to be initiated. If you're already baptized, it's your decision to join the Church that is accepted. The assembly voices its approval.

2. The bishop asks if you're ready for election. You say "yes" and give your name, which is written in the Book of the Elect presented at this rite.

3. You are proclaimed "members of the elect, to be initiated into the sacred mysteries at the next Easter Vigil." Intercessory prayers and a blessing follow.

The Scrutinies (for the Unbaptized Only)

These rites deepen your faith as you think and talk over the meaning of stories from the Gospel of John, read at Mass on three Sundays in Lent.

- The first scrutiny gives us the story of the Samaritan woman at the well (John 4:1–26).

- The second scrutiny focuses on the story of the man born blind (John 9).

- The third scrutiny is the raising of Lazarus (John 11:1–44).

Each Sunday, after the intercessory prayers, the priest prays that you may be freed from the powers of sin.

"Whoever drinks the water I shall give will never thirst."

John 4:14

- *Your relationship with the Lord is changing as you seek him more fully. How is the RCIA helping you in this ongoing conversion?*

Rites of Preparation

Rites of preparation literally prepare you for the core part of your faith journey: receiving the sacraments of initiation. In some RCIA programs, the elect come together to share their thoughts and pray on Holy Saturday before the Easter Vigil. This is another chance to experience the **presentation of the Creed** or the **presentation of the Lord's Prayer**, if you haven't before.

Rites of Initiation

This can be the most emotional part of your faith journey; so much has changed inside you and your parish, all leading up to you receiving baptism, confirmation, and Eucharist during the Easter Vigil celebration.

The vigil of the early Church was once an all-night experience, but today it only lasts a few hours. You have given yourself over to belief in the Father, the Son, and the Holy Spirit, and now you come fully into the Church. It's intense! Here's what you can expect:

1. The celebration starts in darkness (and sometimes outdoors), where a fire is blessed, and then the Easter candle is blessed and ignited with this fire.

2. The priest—with a deacon, if the parish has one—leads the procession into the church as the "Light of Christ" is proclaimed. Tapers held by the people are lit from the Easter candle, illuminating the scene of filling pews.

3. We hear the "Exsultet," a powerful hymn of praise reflecting on all that God has done for us. Now his Son, "breaking the prison bars of death," is gloriously resurrected, and we are redeemed from sin. For the first time since before Lent, we hear the "Gloria."

4. Several Old Testament readings take us through salvation history, alternating with psalms.

5. We listen to a passage from Romans.

6. The "Alleluia" is sung, and we hear the Gospel—Jesus is risen—and the homily.

"One Lord, one faith, one baptism."

Ephesians 4:5

Now it's time to be baptized!

7. You are called forward. In the ancient Litany of the Saints, you hear the names of many saints called on to pray for you.

8. The baptismal water is blessed by the priest, and you are baptized.

9. Next, you are clothed in a white garment, a sign of your sinless new beginning.

10. The rest of the congregation renews their baptismal vows and are sprinkled by the celebrant with the newly blessed waters of baptism.

Now it's your turn:

11. Aloud, you state your belief in the holy catholic Church, joining those just baptized.

12. All of you receive the sacrament of confirmation, including the laying on of hands and the anointing with chrism oil.

13. Finally, you, a new Catholic, help lead the congregation to the Eucharist. You come to the table of the Lord and receive the Body and Blood of Christ for the first time.

14. The priest sends the church out to keep walking the road with the Lord and to bring his message to the community.

Have participants use the timeline below to represent their journey of faith.

There may not be enough space for the timeline on the student handout itself. Encourage participants to use their prayer journal or another sheet of paper so they have the space they need. If you have time, you can let students share their timeline in small groups.

Journey of Faith for Teens: Catechumenate, C1 (826290)
Imprimi Potest: Stephen T. Rehrauer, CSsR, Provincial, Denver Province, the Redemptorists.
Imprimatur: "In accordance with CIC 827, permission to publish has been granted on March 23, 2016, by the Most Reverend Edward M. Rice, Auxiliary Bishop, Archdiocese of St. Louis. Permission to publish is an indication that nothing contrary to Church teaching is contained in this work. It does not imply any endorsement of the opinions expressed in the publication, nor is any liability assumed by this permission."
Journey of Faith © 2000, 2016 Liguori Publications, Liguori, MO 63057. To order, visit Liguori.org or call 800-325-9521. Liguori Publications, a nonprofit corporation, is an apostolate of the Redemptorists. To learn more about the Redemptorists, visit Redemptorists.com. All rights reserved. No part of this publication may be reproduced, distributed, stored, transmitted, or posted in any form by any means without prior written permission.
Contributing writer: Gretchen L. Schwenker, PhD. Editors of 2016 *Journey of Faith:* Theresa Nienaber and Pat Fosarelli, MD, DMin. Design: Lorena Mitre Jimenez.
Images: Shutterstock. Unless noted, Scripture texts in this work are taken from *New American Bible*, revised edition © 2010, 1991, 1986, 1970 Confraternity of Christian Doctrine, Washington, D.C., and are used by permission of the copyright owner. All Rights Reserved. No part of *New American Bible* may be reproduced in any form without permission in writing from the copyright owner. Excerpts from English translation of the *Catechism of the Catholic Church for the United States of America* © 1994 United States Catholic Conference, Inc. —Libreria Editrice Vaticana; English translation of the *Catechism of the Catholic Church: Modifications from the Editio Typica* © 1997 United States Catholic Conference, Inc. —Libreria Editrice Vaticana. Compliant with *The Roman Missal, Third Edition.*
Printed in the United States of America. 20 19 18 17 16 / 5 4 3 2 1. Third Edition.

ISBN 978-0-7648-2629-0

Liguori PUBLICATIONS
A Redemptorist Ministry

Journaling

In his address for the thirtieth World Youth Day in 2015, Pope Francis discussed the sixth beatitude from the Gospel of Matthew: "Blessed are the clean of heart, for they will see God" (5:8). He talked about achieving this through the way we live, especially helping others: "A pure heart is necessarily one which has been stripped bare, a heart that knows how to bend down and share its life with those most in need."

As you seek new life in the Catholic faith, how will you share it with those who need it most, both friends and strangers?

Closing Prayer

After gathering special intentions from the group, pray the Our Father. This familiar prayer proclaims oneness in God, faithfulness to his will, and frequent nourishment as he leads us along the path of faith.

Take-home

Before your next meeting, ask participants to make sure to mark all class meetings and major events of your RCIA process in their calendar, whatever form that takes. Remind them to leave enough time to reflect on and enjoy the journey.

C2: The Sacraments: An Introduction

Catechism: 1084, 1087, 113–34, 1210–12, 1420–21, 1533–35

Objectives

- Define the sacraments as tangible signs of divine love.
- List the seven official sacraments recognized by the Church.
- Identify Christ as instituting the sacraments.
- Define sacraments as different from magic or empty ritualism.

Leader Meditation

Matthew 28:16–20

Jesus promises, "I am with you always, to the end of the age." Through the sacraments, there are visible signs of the Lord's presence in the Church and in our lives. Each sacrament we receive not only increases the Lord's presence but also increases our own awareness of that presence. We don't walk our journey of faith alone. Jesus walks with us every step of the way.

Leader Preparation

- Read the lesson, this lesson plan, the Scripture passage, and the *Catechism* sections. Be prepared to respond to concerns surrounding sacramental doctrine and practice.
- Doing something special for your class this week or inviting the parish outreach or hospitality team to do so would fit with this lesson's message. Candy or other inexpensive gifts would demonstrate that outward signs express invisible realities—like the parish's ongoing support.
- Be familiar with the vocabulary term for this lesson: sacrament. The definition is provided in this guide's glossary.

Welcome

Greet participants as they arrive. Check for supplies and immediate needs. Solicit questions or comments about the previous session and/or share new information and findings. Begin promptly.

Opening Scripture

Matthew 28:16–20

Ask a volunteer to light the candle and read aloud. Following the reading, ask the participants to name ways that Jesus is "with us always...." Before beginning your discussion of the lesson handout, ask participants: ***How do visible and tangible signs of God's love and presence strengthen your faith?***

> Sacraments are "powers that come forth" from the Body of Christ, which is ever-living and life-giving. They are actions of the Holy Spirit at work in his Body, the Church.
>
> *CCC 1116*

In Short:

- Sacraments are tangible signs of divine love.
- The Church recognizes seven official sacraments.
- Christ instituted the sacraments.
- Sacraments are different from magic or empty ritualism.

The Sacraments: An Introduction

Do you remember the first time you were handed the keys to your family car? If it hasn't happened yet, are you looking forward to that day when you'll be able to drive yourself? It's exciting!

But it's not really the keys or the car that makes it that way. Those things are symbols, outward signs of something more important. When you hold those keys, what it really means is:

You have freedom.
You now have the ability to go just about anywhere (with your parents' permission).

You have new power and responsibility.
It may not seem like it, but controlling a car gives you a lot of power. And that means you're also responsible for using it safely.

You have your parents' trust.
When your parents hand you those car keys, they're telling you, "You have earned our trust and confidence. We believe you'll use your best judgment when driving and that you're responsible enough to make good choices."

What Are the Sacraments?

Just like car keys represent privilege and freedom, sacraments are outward signs and actions that represent God's love, saving grace, and presence in our lives. We are physical beings. We learn and understand best through our senses (sight, sound, taste, smell, and touch). We communicate through these senses, too.

For example, if you want to show someone you care, you might use words (which are heard or seen), hugs (which are felt), flowers (which are seen and smelled), or candy (which is seen and tasted). While these physical expressions of love aren't the same as love itself, you communicate your love through them. Words, gestures, and physical objects become signs of love that couldn't be seen otherwise.

How Does Jesus Communicate Love?

Just like we sometimes express our love through symbols, one of the ways Jesus shows his love for us is through the sacraments. Jesus realized that humans needed physical signs to comprehend the incredible reality of his love. While on earth with his disciples, he frequently used physical signs to communicate his love.

CCC 1084, 1087, 113–34, 1210–12, 1420–21, 1533–35

TEENS

The Sacraments: An Introduction

- After reading the introductory text, discuss the meaning of the word *symbol*. Ask participants to name and explain other symbols in their lives.

How does Jesus Communicate Love?

- Discuss why Jesus uses physical signs (sacraments) to express his love for us.

Suggested responses include: He realized we needed physical signs to comprehend the reality of his love.

- Discuss why sacraments are an important part of our faith.

Suggested responses include: The sacraments make the grace of God present to us through the Holy Spirit; the sacraments bring life to the whole Church; the sacraments strengthen us as individuals.

- List and discuss some common sacramental symbols. Discuss why these physical symbols are important for each sacrament (this will be discussed in more detail in later lessons).

Suggested responses include:

- Baptism
  water symbolizes that we are reborn of water and Spirit; sacred chrism signifies the gifts of the Holy Spirit; the white garment symbolizes that you have put on Christ; the Easter candle signifies that you have been enlightened by Christ. (*CCC* 1238–43)

- Confirmation
  anointing with oil signifies the seal of the Holy Spirit and our belonging to Christ; extended hands in blessing has signified the gift of the Spirit since the time of the apostles; a flame signifies the Holy Spirit as it descended onto the apostles on Pentecost. (*CCC* 1296–99)

- The Eucharist
  the Body and Blood re-present the sacrifice of Christ on the cross. (*CCC* 1366)

- Penance
  the sign of the cross and absolution by the priest is the concrete sign that God has forgiven our sins.

- Anointing of the Sick
  the laying on of hands and anointing with oil indicate the graces the sick person receives. (*CCC* 1519–32)

- Matrimony
  exchange of rings is a sign of the couple's love and fidelity.

- Holy Orders
  anointing with holy chrism symbolizes the Holy Spirit; the paten and chalice symbolize a priest is called to present God; giving a deacon the Gospels symbolizes his mission to proclaim the gospel of Christ. (*CCC* 1574)

- Further discuss each of the seven sacraments. Emphasize which are sacraments of initiation, healing, or service and why.

Suggested responses include: Baptism, confirmation, and the Eucharist are sacraments of initiation because they prepare us to enter into the life of the Church. Penance and the anointing of the sick are sacraments of healing because through them God heals our souls and bodies. Matrimony and holy orders are sacraments of service because they prepare us to live our vocation out in the world.

If you have time, go over the listed Gospel passages as a group, or assign participants to work on one passage in a small group.

Suggested responses include:

- Matthew 8:1–3
  He stretched out his hand, touched the leper, cured his leprosy.

- Mark 10:13–16
  Shaking the dust off your feet if they do not listen to your words.

- Luke 9:12–17
  He blessed and broke the bread, multiplied the loaves and fishes.

- John 13:3–5
  He washed the disciples' feet.

Can we look at sacraments in another way?

- Discuss sacraments as divine encounters. Emphasize that this kind of sacrament is very personal.

- Give participants time to answer the reflection question on their own.

Where did the seven official sacraments come from?

- Clarify for participants that the origin of the sacraments is not the Church. Jesus instituted the sacraments here on earth and the Church carries them on.

- Clarify the difference between the rituals we use in the sacraments and other kinds of rituals (like wearing specific socks on game day). Ask participants to compare and contrast these different kinds of rituals.

Suggested response include: The rituals in the sacraments are symbols for the greater, invisible graces God bestows on us through the Holy Spirit. While wearing specific socks on game day might feel like it helps you win, those socks don't actually give you the skill to win the game.

If you have time, you can ask participants to share the ritual they wrote about in the lesson.

Look up one or two of these Gospel passages and write down the physical sign Jesus used to help his followers understand how much he cared for them:

Matthew 8:1–3	Mark 10:13–16
Luke 9:12–17	John 13:3–5

Jesus still uses physical signs to communicate his love for us today in the signs and actions we call the sacraments. The **sacraments** are the saving actions of Christ happening right now for us, his beloved children. The *Catechism of the Catholic Church* helps us to understand this a little better. It tells us that the sacraments are visible signs instituted, or established, by Christ, through which the life of God is given to us. These visible signs and actions make the grace of God present to us through the Holy Spirit (*CCC* 1131).

The Holy Spirit prepares us for the sacraments through the word of God, and we must receive the sacraments with open and loving hearts. If we don't do anything to actively prepare for the sacraments or if our minds and hearts are closed, we won't be able to receive God's grace and love. Even God can't give us a gift we refuse to take.

> *"The visible rites by which the sacraments are celebrated signify and make present the graces proper to each sacrament. They bear fruit in those who receive them with the required dispositions."*
>
> *CCC* 1131

While the sacraments benefit us as individuals, they also bring life to the entire Church. As members of Christ's body, when we are strengthened as individuals, the family of God is strengthened as a whole (*CCC* 1134).

There are seven traditional Catholic sacraments. Baptism, confirmation, and the Eucharist are known as the sacraments of initiation. Reconciliation and the anointing of the sick are known as sacraments of healing because through them God heals our bodies and souls. Lastly, marriage and holy orders are sacraments of service. They prepare us to live out our vocation in the world.

Can We Look at Sacraments in Another Way?

Many of today's Church scholars (those who closely study and help us understand Church teachings) look at sacraments in a second sense. Any person, event, or thing through which you meet God or experience the presence of God is a kind of sacrament.

For example, the first time you climb a mountain and look down at the world below, you might feel God's presence and majesty in a way never experienced before. In a sense, the magnificent beauty of creation you behold in this moment becomes an individual, divine encounter. You are encountering God in a physical way.

Similarly, when your sadness is lessened by the comfort of a caring friend, your friend becomes an experience of God in your time of need. Both the mountains and the friend make God something we can see, hear, touch, and feel.

- *How have you experienced these types of sacraments in your life?*

Where Did the Seven Official Sacraments Come From?

The sacraments began with the human experience of the followers of Jesus. As Jesus' followers grew to know him, they also grew to know God. Jesus himself was sacrament for his disciples. It was through him and him alone that they came to know God (see John 8:19; 14:6–10).

In sharing the good news, the early Christians acted just like their Hebrew ancestors. So future generations wouldn't forget, the Hebrews told and retold important stories, always in the same pattern. These stories contained particular words, rich symbols, and important actions. When specific words and symbolic actions are used over and over again, in the same pattern, the words and actions are called rituals.

• Describe a ritual in your household. This can be how you celebrate birthdays or holidays or something only your family does.

The disciples knew the story of Jesus' baptism: God proclaimed Jesus "beloved Son," and the Spirit came down upon him. This became the foundation of baptism. Under the guidance of the Holy Spirit, the apostles initiated this sacrament, which both symbolized what was happening to them and made God's Spirit present to them in a real way. They were also beginning a new life as sons and daughters of God and receiving the wonderful gift of the Spirit! This is how we experience baptism today.

The early Christians also remembered how Jesus often invited everyone to come and eat with him. We know the Last Supper became the most important of Jesus' shared meals. After the meal he commanded them to remember these events and do as he had done. So the ritual of "breaking bread" and sharing it with others became very important to the disciples. That breaking of the bread became the Eucharist. When the Holy Spirit descended upon the apostles at Pentecost (Acts 2:1–13), it provided them with the necessary graces to go out and evangelize. These same graces are available to us through the sacrament of confirmation. While the Holy Spirit doesn't descend on us in a literal tongue of fire, he still becomes present to us through the symbols and actions of confirmation.

In these and other ways, they continued what Jesus had done. They prayed and laid hands on one another, healed, and forgave, just as they had seen Jesus pray and lay hands on, heal, and forgive. As Jesus had been the sacrament of God for them, they—as members of his Church—were becoming the sacrament of Jesus for others.

Today, as members of Christ's Church, we continue the ritual actions of the first Christians. Just as Jesus used his physical body to bring people closer to God, the risen Lord now uses the seven special rituals we call the sacraments to help us feel, see, and know the presence of God. One very important reason why the Church exists (the Church's mission) is to make Christ truly present in a way that we can feel and understand.

How Do These Seven Sacraments Work?

The sacraments, through symbolic actions, bring about what they symbolize. For example, the ritual of baptism (which involves a person being submerged in water or having water poured over his or her head) symbolizes the person being cleansed of original sin and being filled with the life of the Spirit. At the same time, God is actually making that cleansing happen. This is what makes a sacrament more than just a ritual—God is really present in a sacrament.

We may not feel any different when receiving a sacrament for many reasons. It's possible we've never had the opportunity of experiencing the sacraments as they were meant to be. Or our hearts weren't open to the many ways God works in our lives. As we discussed earlier in this lesson, God can't give us a gift that we aren't open to receiving.

We also may not feel God's presence and action in the sacraments because we're expecting something magical. There is no magic in the sacraments. For example, the water of baptism is just water; there is no magic in it or in the words spoken by the priest. God is beyond magic.

An open heart allows God to act in and through us in ways we never imagined! An open heart does not manipulate God. There was no magic in the way the Church's sacraments began. The sacraments grew out of real-life experiences and the influence of the Holy Spirit. The early disciples wished to spread the good news that their Lord and Savior wasn't gone—he was with them every moment. The sacraments are Christ's loving gift of himself to his Church.

How do these seven sacraments work?

• Emphasize for participants that sacraments aren't a form of magic. For the sacraments to give us the grace they hold, we have to receive them with an open heart and mind, as well as with great faith and trust in God.

Reinforce the difference between the Church's seven sacraments and sacraments as divine encounters. With participants in groups, or as a class, create a visual (a chart, diagram, or image) to explain the differences and similarities between these two kinds of sacraments.

Suggested response include:

Differences: The seven sacraments are community-based and divine encounters are personal; the Church's sacraments use specific signs and rituals; the Church's sacraments usually require a priest to witness or perform the sacrament.

Similarities: Both are talked about in Scripture; both communicate God's love for us; and both help us grow in faith and love.

With a partner or as a group, create a visual (a chart, diagram, or image) to help explain the differences and similarities between a sacrament of the Church (the seven celebrated by the Church) and a sacrament as an individual, divine encounter.

Describe a person or experience that has given you the opportunity to know God a little better.

Is this a person who helps you feel the caring compassion of God? A place so magnificent you begin to understand God's creative power? This coming week, try to become more aware of these moments. Keep a record of them to help you remember.

CATECHUMENATE

JOURNEY OF FAITH

Journey of Faith for Teens: Catechumenate, C2 (826290)
Imprimi Potest: Stephen T. Rehrauer, CSsR, Provincial, Denver Province, the Redemptorists.
Imprimatur: "In accordance with CIC 827, permission to publish has been granted on March 23, 2016, by the Most Reverend Edward M. Rice, Auxiliary Bishop, Archdiocese of St. Louis. Permission to publish is an indication that nothing contrary to Church teaching is contained in this work. It does not imply any endorsement of the opinions expressed in the publication, nor is any liability assumed by this permission."
Journey of Faith © 2000, 2016 Liguori Publications, Liguori, MO 63057. To order, visit Liguori.org or call 800-325-9521. Liguori Publications, a nonprofit corporation, is an apostolate of the Redemptorists. To learn more about the Redemptorists, visit Redemptorists.com. All rights reserved. No part of this publication may be reproduced, distributed, stored, transmitted, or posted in any form by any means without prior written permission.
Text: Adapted from *Journey of Faith* © 2000 Liguori Publications. Editors of 2016 *Journey of Faith:* Theresa Nienaber and Pat Fosarelli, MD, DMin. Design: Lorena Mitre Jimenez. Images: Shutterstock. Unless noted, Scripture texts in this work are taken from *New American Bible*, revised edition © 2010, 1991, 1986, 1970 Confraternity of Christian Doctrine, Washington, D.C., and are used by permission of the copyright owner. All Rights Reserved. No part of *New American Bible* may be reproduced in any form without permission in writing from the copyright owner. Excerpts from English translation of the *Catechism of the Catholic Church* for the United States of America © 1994 United States Catholic Conference, Inc. —*Libreria Editrice Vaticana;* English translation of the *Catechism of the Catholic Church: Modifications from the Editio Typica* © 1997 United States Catholic Conference, Inc. —*Libreria Editrice Vaticana.* Compliant with *The Roman Missal, Third Edition.*
Printed in the United States of America. 20 19 18 17 16 / 5 4 3 2 1. Third Edition.

Liguori PUBLICATIONS
A Redemptorist Ministry

Journaling

Describe a person or experience that has given you the opportunity to know God a little better.

Closing Prayer

After praying for special intentions from the group, pray the Glory Be (Doxology). This simple prayer proclaims God's faithful presence in our lives—yesterday, today, and tomorrow.

Take-home

Before next class, encourage participants to talk to their sponsor or another parishioner about why the sacramental life of the Church is a blessing to him or her.

C3: The Sacrament of Baptism

Catechism: 1229–1233, 1247–1249

Objectives

- Outline the history and biblical foundations of baptism.
- Describe the meaning and effects of baptism.
- Recall several symbols of baptism and their significance.
- Identify the steps of the rite of baptism.

Leader Meditation

Mark 1:4–11

Most of us can't recall our own baptisms. Yet many times along our journey, we review and remake the promises made for us by our godparents. In preparation for this lesson, renew your baptismal promises and pray for the grace and strength to become all that God has created you to become.

Leader Preparation

- Read the lesson, this lesson plan, the Scripture passage, and the *Catechism* sections.
- Have a copy of the baptismal promises to reflect upon for a closing prayer.
- Be familiar with the vocabulary term for this lesson: chrism. The definition is provided in this guide's glossary.

Welcome

Greet participants as they arrive. Check for supplies and immediate needs. Solicit questions or comments about the previous session and/or share new information and findings. Begin promptly.

Opening Scripture

Mark 1:4–11

Ask a volunteer to light the candle and read aloud. Before beginning your discussion of the lesson handout, ask participants to think about ***what elements stand out in this description of Jesus' baptism.***

The faith required for Baptism is not a perfect and mature faith, but a beginning that is called to develop. The catechumen or the godparent is asked: "What do you ask of God's Church?" The response is: Faith. *CCC 1253*

In Short:

- History and biblical foundations of baptism
- Meaning and effects of baptism
- Significance of baptismal symbols
- The rite of baptism

The Sacrament of Baptism

"One Easter I had a chance to meet with a tribe called the Tubolis who live high up in the mountains of Mindanao. For the Easter Vigil, the community of the baptized [Christians] gathered on one side of the river, which is not very wide but very swift and extremely cold. It was dusk, so they had torches; they also had a lot of blankets and a number of jars of oil. Meanwhile, the catechumens, those who were to be baptized, were on the other side of the river. Fr. Rex, their missionary, had planted himself in the middle of the stream, and the rushing water came to just above his waist. Then the community started beckoning to those on the other bank, calling each by name: 'Come on over, Juan; come on over, Maria.'

"The catechumens looked at that stream, and they were a bit fearful because of its swiftness and also because they were already cold. One by one they would plunge into the water with everybody still calling to them. When they came up the other side after being baptized, the community would grab them with blankets, rub oil on them, and pull them into their midst. The whole thing was a powerful scene, and afterward they had a Eucharist, right

there on the banks of the river with the newly baptized."—*Passionist Fr. Donald Senior on his experience in the Philippines*

The word *baptize* comes from a Greek word meaning to plunge or immerse. These words suggest the use of water—an important symbol in the sacrament of baptism. In Fr. Senior's story, the catechumens quite literally plunged into the river, immersing themselves in the water. They then rose on the opposite bank, where they were greeted by and welcomed into the community of believers. Though the Tubolis live half a world away, their experience of the sacrament of baptism is not completely unlike the experience of our catechumens entering the Church on Holy Saturday night.

In both celebrations, darkness is dispelled by the light of a fire—a powerful symbol of Christ's presence. The baptism itself involves the symbols of water and oil. Both experiences also include the active presence of the community of baptized believers who witness the triumphant moment and welcome the newly baptized into their midst.

- *What about baptism makes you excited? Nervous?*

What Is the Sacrament of Baptism?

"Jesus called his death and resurrection a baptism: 'There is a baptism with which I must be baptized, and how great is my anguish until it is accomplished!'"

Luke 12:50

TEENS

CCC 1084, 1087, 113–34, 1210–12, 1420–21, 1533–35

The Sacrament of Baptism

- After reading about the Tuboli baptism ritual, discuss the symbols and gestures we share.

Suggested responses include: We also use water, fire in the form of lit candles, and oil during the sacrament of baptism. Baptism and Eucharist take place among the parish community, not in isolation. The parish community works to support the faith journey of those in the RCIA.

- Talk about the meaning of the word *baptize*. How else are we "plunged" or "immersed" during the sacrament?

What is the Sacrament of Baptism

- As you discuss the sacrament of baptism, emphasize to participants that, even after receiving the sacrament of baptism, we must choose to live good lives. While baptism gives us special graces, even those who have been baptized struggle with a desire toward sin. We are able to live as Christ in the world through discipline, returning to the sacraments of penance and Eucharist, a heartfelt desire to live as God wants, and the willingness to let God move in our lives.

Baptism: A private or community affair?

- Give participants time to think about the reflection question on their own.

- Emphasize that baptism is a sacrament that involves the community of believers as well as the person being baptized. Discuss with participants why this is important or how this influences our attitude toward others.

- Discuss why those baptized in another Christian faith tradition do not have to be rebaptized in the Catholic Church. You can refer them to the section of the *Catechism* on baptism that starts at 1213. You can also cite Ephesians 4:5, which states that there is "one Lord, one faith, one baptism."

The *Catechism* tells us more about the sacrament of baptism and helps us understand Jesus' words. The catechumen's "plunging" into the waters of baptism symbolizes his or her burial into Christ's death. As the catechumen rises from the water, he or she is resurrected with Christ as "a new creature" (CCC 1214). While not as dramatic, the symbolism remains the same when water is poured over the heads of the catechumens.

Perhaps St. Gregory of Nazianzus describes the sacrament of baptism most beautifully:

Baptism is God's most beautiful and magnificent gift....We call it gift, grace, anointing, enlightenment, garment of immortality, bath of rebirth, seal, and most precious gift. It is called gift because it is conferred on those who bring nothing of their own....It is our guard and the sign of God's Lordship.

CCC 1216

In his Letter to the Romans, St. Paul says,

"We know that Christ, raised from the dead, dies no more; death no longer has power over him. As to his death, he died to sin once and for all; as to his life, he lives for God. Consequently, you too must think of yourselves as [being] dead to sin and living for God in Christ Jesus."

Romans 6:9–11

Saint Paul is telling us that we must be imitators of Christ—we must do as Christ did. Rather than a simple ritual, baptism marks the beginning of a deep relationship with the risen Lord.

The baptized person lives "in Christ." As Christians, we have to choose to live good, loving lives. This won't always be easy. We will have our own crosses to bear. We will be tempted to sin. Even so, we must choose to act as Jesus would want us to act. There are no shortcuts to this resurrection with Christ.

While there is no magic, we are strengthened by the Holy Spirit, whose power God promises at the moment of our baptism. A person enters into Christ when they are baptized. That means they also receive the gift of the spirit.

"For those who are led by the Spirit of God are children of God. For you did not receive a spirit of slavery to fall back into fear, but you received a spirit of adoption, through which we cry, "Abba, Father!" The Spirit itself bears witness with our spirit that we are children of God, and if children, then heirs, heirs of God and joint heirs with Christ, if only we suffer with him so that we may also be glorified with him."

Romans 8:14–17

Baptism: A Private or Community Affair?

For Christians, community has always been an important part of life, maybe even the most important part. From the very beginning, God knew that good relationships with other human beings were essential to human happiness. While things may give us pleasure, they aren't a source of lasting happiness. True human happiness comes only through loving relationships with God and others.

> - *Think about your relationships with others. When you're at peace with your parents, do you feel more at peace with yourself? When you feel connected to your friends, do you feel greater contentment?*

For this reason, Christians have always placed great importance on the community of Christ. Christ is at the center, and the community is built around him. Through baptism, we become members of the body of Christ. We begin to share in the privileges and in the life of this community of believers.

While many Catholics still tend to regard baptism as a private family affair, it is truly a sacrament that involves the entire faith community. When we witness a baptism, our own faith should be strengthened and renewed. Every newly baptized person brings unique beauty and special gifts to the body of Christ.

> *"Baptism is the sacrament of faith. But faith needs the community of believers. It is only within the faith of the church that each of the faithful can believe."*
>
> CCC 1253

Because the Catholic Church regards the sacrament of baptism as permanent, it can't be repeated. Baptism causes us to belong to Christ, and that belonging can never be taken away (CCC 1272). Baptism in other Christian faiths is essentially the same as the New Testament practice, which is the basis of Catholic baptism. This makes baptism a bond of unity among all Christians. For this reason, non-Catholic Christians who wish to join the Catholic Church aren't baptized unless there is real doubt as to whether they were ever baptized.

- *How might knowing we are united as family in Christ with all Christians in baptism change how you treat others?*

What Happens To People Who Aren't Baptized?

In the case of adults and children who are not baptized, Catholics believe that God's mercy works in a way not yet revealed to us. Catholics also believe in "baptism of blood" (suffering death for Christ before baptism) and "baptism of desire." Baptism of desire refers to those who "through no fault of their own, do not know the Gospel of Christ... yet sincerely seek God and, moved by grace, strive by their deeds to do his will as it is known to them" (Dogmatic Constitution on the Church [*Lumen Gentium*], 16).

Catholics believe that children who are not baptized are given to the "mercy of God" and "Jesus' tenderness toward children" (CCC 1261), which gives hope for their eternal happiness in heaven.

What Are the Signs of Baptism?

The sign in baptism is the pouring of water, or the immersion in water, along with the words, "I baptize you in the name of the Father, and of the Son, and of the Holy Spirit."

The waters of baptism remind us that Christ has washed us clean of sin and brought us home to God. In baptism, all our sins are washed away. That is why our baptismal promises include a rejection of our sinful ways and a profession of our personal faith.

The usual minister of the baptism ritual is a priest or deacon, but anyone may baptize if someone is in danger of dying. That person is not baptized again if he or she should recover.

Godparents place a white garment on the newly baptized to show that they have become a new creation and have clothed themselves in Christ. A candle is then lit from the Easter candle and is presented to each of those just baptized. This symbolizes that Christ, the Light of the World, is their light, too. And as Paul says, they must now "live as children of light" (Ephesians 5:8).

If baptism is celebrated separate from confirmation, the newly baptized are then anointed with oil. The oil, called **chrism**, is a perfumed oil consecrated (set apart as sacred) by the bishop. The anointing with sacred chrism is a sign that "[God] has also put his seal upon us and given the Spirit in our hearts as a first installment" (2 Corinthians 1:22). The newly baptized now share in the prophetic, kingly, and priestly power of Christ.

- *Can you find examples of God using water, light (fire), or oil as special symbols in the Bible?*

What are the signs of Baptism?

- Discuss the importance of water in the sacrament of baptism. Why is water the perfect symbol of new life?

Suggested responses include: Water is symbolic of the cleansing that takes place during baptism. Christ washes us free from sin and, through baptism, both original sin and all our personal sins are washed away.

- Discuss the importance of the sign (the pouring of water or the immersion into water) and the words, "I baptize you in the name of the Father…."

Suggested responses include: The pouring or immersion remind us that our sins are being washing away. Through the invocation of the Holy Trinity the Church "asks God that through his Son the power of the Holy Spirit may be sent upon the water" (CCC 1239). The importance of the Trinity can be emphasized by pouring water over the baptized three times, or submerging him or her in water three times.

- Discuss the meaning and importance of the sacred chrism, the white garment, and the Easter candle.

Suggested responses include: The sacred chrism becomes the physical sign of the gift of the Holy Spirit; the white garment symbolizes that the newly baptized have "put on Christ" and risen with Christ; the Easter candle symbolizes the light of Christ in the world and the newly baptized's call to go out and be a light to the world.

- As a group or with partners, have students find examples of water, light (fire), or oil used as symbols in the Bible. You may also want to mention to participants that many of these same symbols are used in the Old Testament but have taken on new meaning with Christ's death and resurrection.

Suggested responses include:

o Water
John 4:13–14 "whoever drinks the water I shall give will never thirst;" Hebrews 10:22 "our hearts sprinkled clean from an evil conscience and our bodies washing in pure water;" John 7:38–39 "rivers of living water will flow from him."

o Light/Fire
Psalm 119:105 "Your word is a lamp for my feet;" Matthew 5:13–15 "You are the light of the world;" Ephesians 5:10–16 "everything exposed by the light becomes visible;" 1 Peter 2:9 "him who called you out of the darkness into his wonderful light."

o Oil
Psalm 45:8 "your God has anointed you with the oil of gladness;" Hebrews 1:5–10 "anointed you with the oil of gladness above your companions;" 1 John 2:27 "the anointing that you received from him remains in you."

Answers to the lesson activity appear below.

(1) *the old life*
    the new Christian life

(2) *chrism*

(3) *the baptized becoming a new creation, clothed in Christ*

(4) *that Christ is our light*

(5) *priest or deacon*

(6) *anyone*

Journaling

Our baptism frees us from the power of sin, makes us members of the body of Christ, fills us with the Holy Spirit, and challenges us to live as "children of light." How can you bring the light of Christ to the people in your life today?

Closing Prayer

As a closing prayer, ask the participants to take turns reading and reflecting upon each of the baptismal promises.

Lord Jesus Christ, give us the grace to fulfill our baptismal promises each day of our lives as we strive to die to self and rise with you. Thank you for this sacrament, for washing away original and personal sin, and for raising us up to a life of grace. Amen.

Take-home

Before the next session, participants should find an opportunity to live out whatever they've listed in their journal prompt.

C4: The Sacrament of Confirmation

Catechism: 1229–1233, 1247–1249

Objectives

- Recognize that through confirmation the Spirit empowers us as disciples and witnesses.
- Consider the significance of the sponsor and the baptismal (saint) name.
- Identify the actions that confer the sacrament of confirmation.

Leader Meditation

Acts 1:8–11 and Acts 8:14–17

We have all witnessed the fulfillment of Jesus' promise to send the Holy Spirit. This Spirit comes, also as promised, with the power to make us witnesses to the whole world. Your witness—that is, your daily love-filled, Christ-centered living—is your most effective tool in passing on the faith to the young people in your care.

Leader Preparation

- Read the lesson, this lesson plan, the Scripture passage, and the *Catechism* sections.
- Be familiar with the vocabulary terms for this lesson: witness, chrism, sponsor. The definitions are provided in this guide's glossary.

Welcome

Greet participants as they arrive. Check for supplies and immediate needs. Solicit questions or comments about the previous session and/or share new information and findings. Begin promptly.

Opening Scripture

Acts 1:8–11 and Acts 8:14–17

Ask for two volunteers to read aloud. Explain to the group that the symbolic action described in Acts 8, the laying on of hands, remains an important part of the confirmation ritual today. Before beginning your discussion of the lesson handout, ask participants to **think about what responsibilities are required by those who receive the Holy Spirit.**

> It must be explained to the faithful that the reception of the sacrament of Confirmation is necessary for the completion of baptismal grace. For "by the sacrament of Confirmation, [the baptized] are more perfectly bound to the Church and are enriched with, a special strength of the Holy Spirit." *CCC 1285*

Journey of Faith

In Short:

- Confirmation makes us disciples and witnesses.
- Your choices of a sponsor and a baptismal name are significant.
- Confirmation includes many actions and symbols.

- *Think of a time someone came through for you when you didn't expect it. How did you feel?*

The Sacrament of Confirmation

How do you think the disciples felt in the days following Jesus' crucifixion and death? They must have been grief-stricken; the man who had loved them and led them, washed their feet, shared their meals, and faithfully taught them was now gone. The disciples must have been confused and unsure of their mission. Saint John says they were so afraid that "the doors were locked, where the disciples were, for fear of the Jews" (John 20:19). These feelings of sadness, heartbreak, confusion, and fear are things we can all relate to.

But Jesus did not abandon his friends. He promised them he would give them the courage they needed to face any fears about serving him. "But you will receive power when the holy Spirit comes upon you, and you will be my witnesses in Jerusalem, throughout Judea and Samaria, and to the ends of the earth" (Acts 1:8). That was a promise that Jesus, of course, kept!

The disciples immediately went out and began to preach the good news, their fear and sadness forgotten.

The sacrament of confirmation bestows these gifts of the Holy Spirit upon us. Like Jesus' first disciples, we are given the courage to bring the good news to our own world. Jesus is still fulfilling his promise of the Holy Spirit through the sacrament of confirmation.

"When the time for Pentecost was fulfilled, they were all in one place together. And suddenly there came from the sky a noise like a strong driving wind, and it filled the entire house in which they were. Then there appeared to them tongues as of fire, which parted and came to rest on each one of them. And they were all filled with the holy Spirit and began to speak in different tongues, as the Spirit enabled them to proclaim."

Acts 2:1–4

The sacraments of baptism, confirmation, and Eucharist are called the sacraments of initiation. These three sacraments lay the foundation for every Christian life. We are born anew through our baptism, strengthened in confirmation, and nourished by the food of eternal life in the Eucharist (CCC 1212).

Because of the close connection between baptism and confirmation, the early Christians usually celebrated the two sacraments together in one rite, although the New Testament does lay a foundation for two different celebrations. (See Acts 8:15, Acts 19:1–7, and Hebrews 6:2.)

TEENS

CCC 1285–1321

The Sacrament of Confirmation

- After reading the introductory paragraphs, ask students to share their response to the reflection question.

- Ask the participants how they feel when the topic of faith is brought up. Is it difficult to talk about? Can they openly proclaim their faith in Jesus or do they prefer to keep it to themselves?

- Discuss what it means to be a witness to faith. Ask for examples of other figures who are examples of strong witness (biblical figures or saints are a good place to start).

Suggested responses include: Being a witness means being active in your faith. It means acknowledging your faith even when it might be dangerous (or it's the unpopular choice). It means taking actions to live more like Christ on earth.

How Is the Sacrament Celebrated?

- Clarify the meaning and importance of the three sacraments of initiation: baptism, confirmation, and Eucharist.

- These three sacraments lay the foundation for every Christian life. We are born anew in baptism, are strengthened through confirmation, and receive the food for eternal life in the Eucharist (*CCC 1212*).

What Is a Sponsor?

- Make a list of all the characteristics of a good sponsor. Encourage participants to use this list when choosing their own.

Suggested responses include: They visibly live the Catholic faith, someone you respect or admire, the time to be your sponsor and provide spiritual direction, someone knowledgeable about the teachings of the Church, someone who is a permanent part of your life, someone with a strong faith, and more.

While the Holy Spirit is given in both baptism and confirmation, the function or work of the Spirit is different in each. At baptism, we are made members of Christ's body, but at confirmation we are given the power of God to bear fruit in our Christian lives. The gifts of the Holy Spirit empower us to live as Jesus taught us to live. Through our love, we build up the Church, the body of Christ.

There's another way to look at the connection between baptism and confirmation. When a baby is born, he or she has the potential to become an active, productive adult, but the baby needs time to mature, develop, and grow. Compare the baby to a newly baptized Christian. The Christian doesn't become a perfect imitator of Christ overnight. The potential is there, but the Christian needs time to mature spiritually. The gifts of the Holy Spirit received at confirmation give us guidance and strength on our journey of faith.

The word *confirmation* means "strengthening." The Holy Spirit comes and strengthens those gifts we received at baptism. The Holy Spirit helps us to mature spiritually so that we can live fully Christian lives. But there's no magic in confirmation and no shortcuts to heaven. The sacraments require our response in the form of Christian witness or action. God offers us the empowering gifts of the Holy Spirit in confirmation, but it's up to us to choose to accept the gifts and use them to the best of our abilities.

To **witness** means to "stand up for the truth," even at the expense of your own life.

Because Christian growth and maturity bring a greater sense of responsibility toward those around us, confirmation is sometimes called "the sacrament of Christian witness" or "the sacrament of social action." Often preparation for this sacrament will include a service project or other activity that focuses on Christian action within the community.

The strengthening and spiritual maturity we gain through confirmation isn't only for our personal benefit. We receive them through the Holy Spirit so we can contribute to the life of the Church and our world.

- What gifts or talents do you have right now that you could use to make the world a better, more joyful place?

How Is the Sacrament Celebrated?

The sacrament of confirmation is given by the laying on of hands, followed by the anointing in the form of a cross with chrism on the forehead. **Chrism** is perfumed oil consecrated (made sacred) by a bishop. It is a sign of the gifts of the Holy Spirit (*CCC 1241*). The oil is a symbol of strength, and the perfume is a symbol of the fragrance of Christ, which the Christian must spread.

The laying on of hands is an important action found in the Bible by which the Holy Spirit is asked to come to a person. In the Gospels, Jesus healed many people with a touch. It makes sense that the power of the Spirit comes through a special touch—the laying on of hands and praying for the gift of the Spirit.

The anointing is another important action. The words *Messiah* and *Christ* both mean "anointed one." The Israelites anointed priests and, later, kings as a sign that they were chosen by God. Like these priests and kings, you are chosen by God. And like them, you are being anointed or chosen for a purpose.

As you are anointed, the minister of the sacrament will say these words: *Be sealed with the gift of the Holy Spirit.*

Usually it is the bishop, the leader of the larger Church community, who administers the sacrament. The bishop witnesses the new Christian's welcome and initiation into the worldwide community of believers.

What Is a Sponsor?

The word **sponsor** comes from the same root as responsible, a root that means "someone who guarantees, pledges, or promises." The idea of having a sponsor comes from the early Church, when Christians lived in fear of being persecuted for their faith. Catechumens—those wishing to become Christians—had to have a sponsor, someone who would vouch for their sincerity.

Although the purpose of the sponsor may have changed, the role remains an important one. A sponsor is a person who can travel with you on your journey to Christian maturity. This person should know you well and be available to listen to your concerns and answer your questions about your faith and the Church. Your sponsor should be a person with whom you intend to have a lifelong relationship. This person must also be mature, belong to the Catholic Church, and have received the three sacraments of initiation: baptism, confirmation, and Eucharist. Perhaps most importantly, your sponsor needs to be a spiritual friend, someone you can talk to about matters of the heart.

> • *By yourself or with the group, make a list of all the characteristics you think it takes to be a good sponsor.*
>
> • *Who are some people you might consider? Why?*

What Does a Sponsor Do?

During confirmation, the sponsor places a hand on the candidate's shoulder as a sign that the sponsor is presenting the candidate for the sacrament on behalf of the whole Christian community. Being a sponsor involves more than just showing up for the confirmation ceremony. It is the sponsor's responsibility to encourage the newly confirmed Christian to be Christ's witness and to bring the light of Christ to the world.

Another tradition of the Church at the time of confirmation is choosing a name that will remind you of this sacrament and its purpose. Your prayerful thought will help you determine that name. You might want to choose the name of a saint who represents the kind of Christian you wish to be. You might want to recommit yourself to your given (baptismal) name, especially after you study its meaning and discover some of the great people in Christian history who have shared it with you. Some candidates choose the name of a relative, close friend, or other person they have deeply admired.

> • *Make a list of all the characteristics of faith you feel are especially important or you need the most help with.*
>
> • *Who are the people who could be your role models in living this list?*

When Is Confirmation Conferred?

The age of confirmation varies within the United States. At one time, young people were confirmed around the age of ten. But that has increased to twelve to seventeen years old because of the commitment it takes to witness to the faith. Confirmation is a sacrament of Christian witness and commitment, and witnessing to the faith requires maturity and a strong understanding of what that means.

Being confirmed means you're committing to the faith, and committing to the faith means you're going to be called as a witness for Christ. That isn't always easy. This is why we have the sacrament of confirmation. Through this sacrament you are anointed with the power of the Holy Spirit to profess your faith and to represent the truth—even to those outside the Church. Through this sacrament you become fully immersed, or completely involved, in the life of the Church.

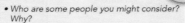

What Does a Sponsor Do?

• Ask participants to share their list of characteristics of faith. Encourage them to use this list when choosing their saint name.

Suggested responses include: Commitment to the teachings of the Church, willingness to witness to your faith, willingness to evangelize and tell others about the faith when appropriate, desire to learn more about the faith, desire to grow closer to God, a strong prayer life, a personal relationship with God the Father, Son, and Holy Spirit, a desire to participate in the sacraments, and so on.

When Is Confirmation Conferred?

• Discuss the ways that confirmation continues or completes our baptism.

• The difference between baptism and confirmation is hinted at by St. Augustine when he explains that in baptism we are mixed with water so that we might take on the form of bread, the Body of Christ. But bread, he points out, needs to be baked in the fire; and this fire is supplied by the chrism which is "the sacrament of the Holy Spirit," who was revealed in tongues of fire.

Answers to the lesson activity appear below.

(1) *initiation*

(2) *baptism and Eucharist*

(3) *presentation or presenting the candidate for the sacrament or presenting the candidate on behalf of the whole Christian community*

(4) *strengthening*

(5) *the Holy Spirit coming to a person*

(6) *Anointed One*

(7) *(you are) chosen for a purpose*

(8) *to have a reminder of the sacrament and purpose or to choose a saint who inspires you to live your Christian witness.*

CATECHUMENATE

JOURNEY OF FAITH

Complete the sentences about confirmation.

Confirmation is one of the three sacraments of _____; the other two are _____ and _____.

During the confirmation rite, the sponsor places a hand on the candidate's shoulder as a sign of _____

The word confirmation means _____

Laying on of hands signifies _____

Messiah and Christ both mean _____

At confirmation, being anointed means _____

The purpose of choosing a confirmation name is _____

Take a moment to read and reflect on Isaiah 11:2–3 from the Hebrew Scriptures.

Think about who you are at this time in your life. Of all the Spirit's special gifts, which do you believe you need the most? Why?

Journey of Faith for Teens: Catechumenate, C4 (826290)
Imprimi Potest: Stephen T. Rehrauer, CSsR, Provincial, Denver Province, the Redemptorists.
Imprimatur: "In accordance with CIC 827, permission to publish has been granted on March 23, 2016, by the Most Reverend Edward M. Rice, Auxiliary Bishop, Archdiocese of St. Louis. Permission to publish is an indication that nothing contrary to Church teaching is contained in this work. It does not imply any endorsement of the opinions expressed in the publication; nor is any liability assumed by this permission."
Journey of Faith © 2000, 2016 Liguori Publications, Liguori, MO 63057. To order, visit Liguori.org or call 800-325-9521. Liguori Publications, a nonprofit corporation, is an apostolate of the Redemptorists. To learn more about the Redemptorists, visit Redemptorists.com. All rights reserved. No part of this publication may be reproduced, distributed, stored, transmitted, or posted in any form by any means without prior written permission.
Text: Adapted from *Journey of Faith* © 2000 Liguori Publications. Editors of 2016 *Journey of Faith*: Theresa Nienaber and Pat Fosarelli, MD, DMin. Design: Lorena Mitre Jimenez. Images: Shutterstock. Unless noted, Scripture texts in this work are taken from *New American Bible*, revised edition. © 2010, 1991, 1986, 1970 Confraternity of Christian Doctrine, Washington, D.C., and are used by permission of the copyright owner. All Rights Reserved. No part of *New American Bible* may be reproduced in any form without permission in writing from the copyright owner. Excerpts from English translation of the *Catechism of the Catholic Church* for the United States of America © 1994 United States Catholic Conference, Inc. —Libreria Editrice Vaticana, English translation of the *Catechism of the Catholic Church: Modifications from the Editio Typica* © 1997 United States Catholic Conference, Inc. —Libreria Editrice Vaticana. Compliant with the Roman Missal, third edition.
Printed in the United States of America. 20 19 18 17 16 / 5 4 3 2 1. Third Edition.

Liguori
PUBLICATIONS
A Redemptorist Ministry

Journaling

Take a moment to read and reflect on Isaiah 11:2–3 from the Old Testament. Think about who you are at this time in your life. Of all the Spirit's special gifts, which do you believe you need the most? Why?

Closing Prayer

Conclude the lesson by reading this excerpt from the *Prayer to the Holy Spirit* (or *Come, Holy Spirit*) and then ask the participants for petitions.

Lord, by the light of the Holy Spirit you have illumined the hearts of your faithful. In the same Spirit help us to relish what is right and always rejoice in your consolation. We ask this through Christ our Lord. Amen.

Looking Ahead

The next session will discuss the final sacrament of initiation, the Eucharist. Before the next session, participants should spend time thinking about how God makes himself present to us in the sacraments and what that means to them.

C5: The Sacrament of the Eucharist

Catechism: 1322–1419

Objectives

- Recognize the scriptural context for Catholic teaching on the Eucharist.
- Relate and reflect on the Real Presence in the Eucharist.
- Identify the call to imitate Christ in being food for others.

Leader Meditation

John 6:25–51

As Catholics, our faith in the Real Presence of our Lord in the Eucharist sets us apart from many other Christian churches. Meditate on this passage from St. John's Gospel, which proclaims the central truth upon which all Catholic truths are based. Our faith must be like that of the apostles, who answered Jesus, saying, "Lord, to whom can we go? You have the words of eternal life" (John 6:68).

Leader Preparation

- Read the lesson, this lesson plan, the Scripture passage, and the *Catechism* sections. This may help you answer questions from participants coming from faith traditions that view holy Communion as only symbolic.
- If possible, try to schedule a time of eucharistic adoration for your RCIA group.
- If you can, bring unconsecrated bread and wine to show participants.
- Be familiar with the vocabulary terms for this lesson: sacrifice, transubstantiation. Definitions are provided in this guide's glossary.

Welcome

Greet participants as they arrive. Check for supplies and immediate needs. Solicit questions or comments about the previous session and/or share new information and findings. Begin promptly.

Opening Scripture

John 6:25–51

Because this reading is lengthy, you may wish to have two or three participants share the reading. Ask the first reader to light the candle prior to proclaiming the word. Before beginning your discussion of the lesson handout, ask participants to think about **what it means for Jesus to be the "bread of life."**

> The holy Eucharist completes Christian initiation. Those who have been raised to the dignity of the royal priesthood by Baptism and configured more deeply to Christ by confirmation participate with the whole community in the Lord's own sacrifice by means of the Eucharist.
>
> *CCC 1322*

In Short:

- The Eucharist has a Scriptural context.
- Jesus is truly present to us in the Eucharist.
- Through the Eucharist we are called to imitate Christ.

- How would your best friends or parents react in this situation?
- Do you think those reactions might change as the meal went on and people got to know each other?

"By this sacrament we unite ourselves to Christ, who makes us sharers in his Body and Blood to form a single body."

CCC 1331

The Sacrament of the Eucharist

Imagine your parents have given you permission to host a summer barbecue in your back yard.

On the evening of the barbecue, your best friends are the first to arrive. They help you prepare the grill and refreshments. They eagerly anticipate the arrival of the rest of the guests so the evening of fun can begin. But when the doorbell rings, your friends seem confused. You haven't invited the usual crowd of kids from school but the ones you and your friends tend to ignore. In walks a young man who once got into trouble for using illegal drugs. With him is another teen whose family lives in a poor part of town. Following them are the kids who don't seem to fit in anywhere; kids who are normally shunned and made fun of.

You greet everyone warmly, shaking hands and offering refreshments. You introduce them to your best friends and your parents. Then you invite everyone to sit down together and enjoy the food.

This might sound strange, but it's exactly what Jesus did in his ministry.

It's part of our nature to want to belong to a group of people whose common interests and values we share. It is, unfortunately, also part of our nature to exclude those we perceive as different or whose behavior we decide is unacceptable. Sometimes we exclude others only because it makes us feel better about ourselves. We all want to be "in" and not "out." This same behavior was part of Jesus' culture when he preached here on earth.

Unlike others in his time, Jesus enjoyed table fellowship with anyone who wished to eat with him. He didn't just eat with his regular followers and best friends—who were themselves simple, uneducated Galilean fishermen—but also with the despised tax collectors and sinners.

Hundreds of years of tradition had given all Jewish formal meals a great religious and social importance. The Jews at that time actually believed that by eating meals with sinners, especially non-Jews, Jesus was offending God. Jesus' choice to welcome outcasts into the community by sharing meals with them

CCC 1285–1321

The Sacrament of the Eucharist

- Discuss the introductory questions together. Ask participants why sharing a meal together has such importance.

Suggested responses include: We share what we have (our food) with others, we get to know people over food and conversation, we invite people into our space (whether at school or at home), and so forth.

What Was Jesus Telling Us Through His Actions?

- Ask participants "What does Jesus' desire to break bread with everyone—even outcasts—tell us about him?"

Suggested responses include: he wants everyone to feel welcome, we are all part of Jesus' family—even sinners, Jesus wants a personal relationship with everyone, Jesus didn't care if people thought he was popular....

- Then give participants time, individually or in groups, to look up one or two instances of Jesus sharing a meal with sinners in the Bible. Allow time for sharing and encourage collecting these passages in a prayer journal or notebook.

Suggested responses include:

  o Matthew 9:10–13: *Jesus eats with tax collectors and sinners.*

  o Mark 2:15–17: *Jesus eats with tax collectors and sinners.*

  o Luke 5:29–32: *Jesus eats with tax collectors and sinners.*

  o Luke 7:36–50: *Jesus dines with a pharisee and the woman comes to wash his feet.*

  o Luke 14:12–14: *Jesus teaches one should invite the poor, crippled, lame, and blind to the table and not one's friends or relatives.*

---

scandalized the Jews of his time. They would have been much less offended had Jesus chosen to become an outcast himself.

> *"While he was at table in his house, many tax collectors and sinners sat with Jesus and his disciples; for there were many who followed him."*
>
> Mark 2:15

What Was Jesus Telling Us Through His Actions?

The Jewish people had long believed that God was on their side, and it was this belief that upheld them through centuries of struggle. Then Jesus came along, claiming that God was also on the side of the outcasts and the non-Jews. Through his words and actions, Jesus let his people know they were mistaken about God's attitude toward those they viewed as outcasts.

Table fellowship, a very important part of Jesus' Jewish culture, was more than sitting down and grabbing a quick meal with someone. Eating carried a great deal of significance. Sitting down and eating with someone was a way of showing your comradery with the person. By sharing table fellowship with people condemned by the Jews, Jesus was preaching forgiveness of sins and the offer of a new kind of relationship with God, as well as a new kind of relationship with all people. Clearly Jesus ate with outcasts not only because he loved them but also because he wanted us to understand the nature of the reign of God. God does not wish salvation and eternal happiness for just one group. God's love is for everyone, and it's our mission to bring this good news to the ends of the earth.

- *Find some instances of Jesus sharing a meal with sinners in the Bible. What can you learn from them?* **?**

The Eucharist as Meal

It was this very important experience of table fellowship that Jesus brought with him to his farewell meal with his friends: the Last Supper. During this meal, Jesus told his most beloved followers: *"This is my body.... This is my blood"* (Matthew 26:26–30). Through the action of the breaking of the bread, Jesus spoke of the New Covenant and of God's forgiveness. He also spoke of the terrible price he must pay so we might live.

This meal was a powerful message for the disciples. If they truly listened to Jesus' words and understood his actions, if they lived up to what this meal required of them, then they—like Jesus—must be ready to lay down their lives for others if called.

The Eucharist as Sacrifice

The Church teaches that the Eucharist is both meal and sacrifice. We have tried to understand how important sharing a meal was to Jesus and to the culture in which he lived. We must also try to understand the meaning of sacrifice in biblical times.

Although we no longer offer sacrifices as people did in the ancient world, during the time of Jesus, Jewish households offered **sacrifices** to God. The offerings were usually something connected with life, such as a living animal or fruits of the harvest. When the living offering was made, the people made an internal offering at the same time. They offered their lives to God's service. The most important part of the sacrifice was what went on in their minds and hearts—the offering of their lives to God.

The Christian community has always believed that Jesus' death on the cross was the greatest of all sacrifices. This is because of what went on in his mind and heart. Jesus succeeded in doing what human beings have always struggled to do; he made an offering of himself.

While the Mass recalls Jesus' offering of himself out of his love for us, it is not attempting to reenact the ancient sacrifices or the execution of Jesus. Christ died only once (Romans 6:9–10). The Mass does re-represent the one sacrifice of Jesus at the Last

---

The Eucharist as Sacrifice

- Discuss how the Eucharist is both a meal and sacrifice.

Suggested responses include:

Just as table fellowship was important in Jesus' culture, it is also important to us as Catholics. By sharing the Eucharist as a meal with our brothers and sisters in Christ, we are showing our camaraderie with each other.

Unlike the Jewish households of Jesus' time who offered sacrifices to God such as animals or fruits of their harvest, Catholics believe Jesus' death on the cross was the ultimate sacrifice. Every

Mass, Jesus is re-presented as that sacrifice. We celebrate the "memorial of his sacrifice" and "offer to the Father what he has himself given us: the gifts of creation" (CCC 1357).

- Discuss in detail the difference between outward appearance and inner reality.

Supper and on the Cross. Through our participation in the Mass and partaking in the Eucharist, this one sacrifice is made present to us. The Mass offers us a chance to dedicate our lives completely to God and to one another. Our offering is our own free will, united with Jesus' ultimate act of will.

> "Faithful to the Lord's command the Church continues to do, in his memory and until his glorious return, what he did on the eve of his Passion."
>
> CCC 1333

The Real Presence of Christ

Catholics believe that when Jesus said, "This is my body....This is my blood," he meant exactly what he said. For Jews at the time of Jesus, body meant the person, and blood was the source of life within the person. So Jesus was saying over the bread and cup, "This is myself." We believe that the consecrated bread and wine truly become the Body and Blood of Christ present in the Eucharist.

The New Testament speaks to the reality of Christ's presence in the Eucharist. Chapter 6 of John's Gospel is devoted to Jesus as the "Bread of Life." Jesus multiplies loaves and fish, a miracle that symbolizes his ability to multiply his presence in the Eucharist.

But most important, Jesus himself tells us:

> "I am the living bread that came down from heaven; whoever eats this bread will live forever; and the bread that I will give is my flesh for the life of the world."
>
> John 6:51, 53

Many of Jesus' followers found these words intolerable and left him. But Jesus did not say, "Wait, I meant that the bread only represents my body." Instead, he asked the Twelve, "Do you also want to leave?" Peter answered, "Master, to whom shall we go? You have the words of eternal life" (John 6:67–68).

Like Peter, Catholics don't claim to understand how bread and wine become Christ's body and blood. We accept, as Peter did, the "words of eternal life" on the authority of Jesus. This has been a firm part of the Christian faith since its beginning.

> "It is by the conversion of the bread and wine into Christ's body and blood that Christ becomes present in this sacrament."
>
> CCC 1375

In the twelfth century, the Church began using the word **transubstantiation** to describe the change from the substance of bread to the substance of the flesh of Christ. The problem is that the modern word substance has a different meaning than its Latin root. When we think of a substance, we think in terms of weight and volume. However, the original meaning of substance had less to do with appearances and more to do with the inner reality of a thing, the deepest level of its being.

Take yourself as an example. You are flesh, bones, muscle, a little fat, lots of water, and so on. But that doesn't describe what you really are. You are a human person, created in God's own image, full of feelings, thoughts, and ideas, and blessed with the uniquely human capacity to love. Your appearance and who you are two distinctly different things.

This is the same with the bread and wine we receive at Mass. While the outer appearances (taste, color, weight) of the bread and wine remain the same before and after the consecration, the inner realities have changed from bread and wine to the Body and Blood of Jesus Christ. This is transubstantiation.

When we receive holy Communion, we receive the whole person of Christ as he is at the present moment, that is, as risen Lord, with his glorified body and his full divinity or godliness. When we hear the priest say to us, "The body of Christ" or "the blood of Christ," our response is "Amen!" In other words, "Let it be so. I believe!"

• How would you describe the presence of Christ in the Eucharist to someone else? Write a response, draw an image, or anything else you can think of.

The Real Presence of Christ

• Emphasize the mystery of the Eucharist and that transubstantiation is a miracle. "The Eucharistic presence of Christ begins at the moment of the consecration and endures as long as the Eucharistic species subsist" (CCC 1377).

• If it's helpful for the group, turn to the section of the Catechism that says, "The presence of Christ by the power of his word and the Holy Spirit," which starts at CCC 373 and read through the official Church teaching on the Real Presence of Christ in the Eucharist.

• Give practical examples of how we become the body of Christ through our participation in the Eucharist. Ask participants to share examples as well.

Suggested responses include: When we provide for those in need, when we make a gift of ourselves by giving our time and attention to someone, when we bear our sufferings patiently...

• Ask participants to create something to explain the Real Presence to someone else (let them be creative) then ask volunteers to share. Clarify any misunderstandings or refer participants to the relevant Catechism sections (CCC 1373–1381).

Answers to the lesson activity appear below.

(1) *meal and sacrifice*

(2) *consecration*

(3) *transubstantiation*

(4) *True*

(5) *Amen*

Journey of Faith for Teens: Catechumenate, C5 (826290)
Imprimi Potest: Stephen T. Rehrauer, CSsR, Provincial, Denver Province, the Redemptorists.
Imprimatur: "In accordance with CIC 827, permission to publish has been granted on March 23, 2016, by the Most Reverend Edward M. Rice, Auxiliary Bishop, Archdiocese of St. Louis. Permission to publish is an indication that nothing contrary to Church teaching is contained in this work. It does not imply any endorsement of the opinions expressed in the publication, nor is any liability assumed by this permission."
Journey of Faith © 2000, 2016 Liguori Publications, Liguori, MO 63057. To order, visit Liguori.org or call 800-325-9521. Liguori Publications, a nonprofit corporation, is an apostolate of the Redemptorists. To learn more about the Redemptorists, visit Redemptorists.com. All rights reserved. No part of this publication may be reproduced, distributed, stored, transmitted, or posted in any form by any means without prior written permission.
Text: Adapted from *Journey of Faith* © 2000 Liguori Publications. Editors of 2016 *Journey of Faith:* Theresa Nienaber and Pat Fosarelli, MD, DMin. Design: Lorena Mitre Jimenez. Images: Shutterstock. Unless noted, Scripture texts in this work are taken from *New American Bible, revised edition* © 2010, 1991, 1986, 1970 Confraternity of Christian Doctrine, Washington, D.C., and are used by permission of the copyright owner. All Rights Reserved. No part of *New American Bible* may be reproduced in any form without permission in writing from the copyright owner. Excerpts from English translation of the *Catechism of the Catholic Church* for the United States of America © 1994 United States Catholic Conference, Inc. —*Libreria Editrice Vaticana;* English translation of the *Catechism of the Catholic Church: Modifications from the Editio Typica* © 1997 United States Catholic Conference, Inc. —*Libreria Editrice Vaticana.* Compliant with *The Roman Missal, Third Edition.*
Printed in the United States of America. 20 19 18 17 16 / 5 4 3 2 1. Third Edition.

Liguori PUBLICATIONS
A Redemptorist Ministry

Journaling

When we share the Body and Blood of Christ with our brothers and sisters in faith, we are both nourished and challenged. Are there times you refuse others a place at your table? Are there ways you can change your actions or attitudes to become more open and accepting?

Closing Prayer

Close this lesson by continuing the reading of John 6. Before reading aloud, explain that many of Jesus' disciples were confused and discouraged by his words. They could not accept his challenge. Read verses 60 through 68, ending with Simon Peter's words, "Lord, to whom can we go? You have the words of eternal life. We have come to believe and know that you are the Holy One of God." Pray:

Lord, help us to take you at your word, to trust when we feel some of the confusion your first disciples felt, and to preserve in the faith that we, too, may come to know the treasure you have given us in your own Body and Blood, broken and poured out for our sins, become for us the food of everlasting life. Amen.

Looking Ahead

Receiving the Eucharist is a great honor and responsibility. Before your next meeting, ask participants to think about how they would prepare themselves to receive a great honor and what that might mean for receiving the Eucharist.

C6: The Sacrament of Penance and Reconciliation

Catechism: 1420–1498

Objectives

- Recognize that no sin is hidden from God.
- Discover sin has consequences beyond the individual.
- Identify the Scriptural roots of penance.
- Outline the basic steps in reconciliation and penance.

Leader Meditation

Luke 15:11–32

As you read the parable of the Prodigal Son, first put yourself in the place of the father. Respond with the father's reaction. Do the same with the older son, and finally with the younger son. Consider how many times you have been placed in similar positions. When have you yearned for forgiveness? When have you been hurt by someone you love deeply?

Leader Preparation

- Read the lesson, this lesson plan, the Scripture passage, and the *Catechism* sections.
- If possible, arrange to have participants see the reconciliation room or confessional area following the lesson.
- Be familiar with the vocabulary terms for this lesson: penance, absolution, reconciliation, examination of conscience. Definitions are provided in this guide's glossary.

Welcome

Greet participants as they arrive. Check for supplies and immediate needs. Solicit questions or comments about the previous session and/or share new information and findings. Begin promptly.

Opening Scripture

Luke 15:11–32

Ask a volunteer to light the candle and read aloud. Have the participants meditate on the feelings experienced by the three central figures in the story. Ask them to imagine the unconditional love this father felt for his lost son. Remind them that this is only a fraction of the love God has for each of us. Before beginning your discussion of the lesson handout, discuss with participants **what it means to be forgiven.**

> Those who approach the sacrament of Penance obtain pardon from God's mercy for the offense committed against [God], and are, at the same time, reconciled with the Church.
>
> *CCC 1422*

In Short:

- Sin isn't hidden from God.
- Sin has consequences beyond yourself.
- Scripture can support penance.
- The sacrament follows several steps.

The Sacrament of Penance and Reconciliation

Elizabeth and Allison had been very good friends since the sixth grade. In their first year of high school, they continued to share everything and were always there for each other.

One evening, they went to the movies with a group of friends. They told their parents where they were going, what they were going to see, and who would be there. But once they got to the theater the rest of the group decided to see another movie—one Elizabeth and Allison knew their parents wouldn't have approved. They were uncomfortable but convinced themselves it wasn't really a problem. After all, they weren't exactly lying to their parents.

When the girls talked the next morning, they debated what story they would tell their parents. They were irritable with one another. Something special about their friendship seemed to be missing. They both felt disconnected from their parents and each other. There were feelings of separation and loneliness inside each of them.

How could one small bad decision suddenly seem so big?

This example shows how one small decision can ripple out into something bigger. Elizabeth and Allison's choice to lie to their parents turned into something that pushed them away from each other, damaging both their relationships with each other and their parents. This small choice with bigger consequences might remind you of the creation story in Genesis. At first, Adam and Eve lived in harmony and peace with themselves, each other, creation, and God. Then the serpent—Satan—entered the Garden of Eden and Adam and Eve sinned. In Genesis 3, we see the pain and alienation they experienced after they disobeyed God.

> *"Sin is an offense against God....Sin sets itself against God's love for us and turns our hearts away from it."*
>
> CCC 1850

Alienation From Self

Alienation means "a feeling of separation or distance." Genesis 3:7 tells us that after Adam and Eve sinned, they experienced feelings of shame and guilt for the first time. They lost respect for themselves. They were suddenly aware of their nakedness, their imperfections, and their selfish side. Feelings of openness and confidence were replaced with feelings of shame.

Alienation From God

Genesis 3:8 goes on to tell us that "the man and his wife hid themselves from the LORD God." The trust and closeness that had been part of their relationship with God was replaced with fear and distance.

The Sacrament of Penance and Reconciliation

- After reading the introduction, ask the participants if they have ever experienced the inner turmoil felt by Elizabeth and Allison.

- While participants might not be able to relate to this exact instance, encourage them to think about a time when a seemingly small, bad choice led to bigger consequences or a hurt relationship.

- Ask participants how sin can result in alienation from self, God, and community.

Suggested responses include:

It alienates us from ourselves because we feel ashamed of or guilty for what we did, we know we've done something wrong and we're embarrassed or frustrated with ourselves, we feel hurt because we've hurt someone we care about...

It alienates us from God because sin is actively pushing away from God and his Word, we might "hide" from God like Adam and Eve did because we're ashamed, we might feel God stopped loving us or won't forgive us so we distance ourselves...

It alienates us from others because we might have hurt someone else who we need to make amends to, we might lash out at others looking for someone else to blame, our bad choices might cause others to pull away from us until we straighten things out...

What Is Sin?

- Ask the participants to define sin in their own words, then discuss the definition of sin provided. Emphasize the beautiful gifts of forgiveness and healing, especially as we receive them through reconciliation and penance.

- If you have time and feel the group would benefit from it, you can read through sections 1468–70 in the *Catechism* as a group. This section is about the effects of reconciliation and might help start your discussion on sin and why forgiveness is important.

How Did Jesus Feel About Sin

- Refer back to the parable of the Prodigal Son, today's opening Scripture. Discuss how this parable shows God's love for us.

- *Suggested responses include: God is like the father who forgave his son, God will always come to meet us when we truly repent....*

- Emphasize how the sacrament of reconciliation and penance is connected to Jesus' ministry.

  o You can remind students of the Scripture passages they looked up in Q5: *The Eucharist,* for how frequently Jesus ate with sinners and how he always had an attitude of mercy toward them.

- Ask participants how Jesus' ministry emphasized mercy and forgiveness. If you have time, ask participants to find Scripture passages that show this.

Often when we sin, we think God must be angry with us. We distance ourselves from God, thinking we are unworthy of his love. It's important for us to remember that we don't (we can't) earn God's love. God's love is an unconditional love. God loves us only for who we are, not for what we do or don't do.

Alienation From Community

"The woman whom you put here with me— she gave me fruit from the tree, so I ate it."

Genesis 3:12

Adam tried to blame Eve for leading him into disobedience, just as Eve blamed the serpent. As a result, Adam and Eve felt a great deal of tension and anger toward each other. We've all experienced selfishness in ourselves and others. Selfish people aren't people we want to be around because it's hard to trust people who only look out for themselves. This is why sin gradually affects everyone close to us. It brings problems and divisions.

- How did Allison and Elizabeth's dishonest behavior affect their relationship with each other? With their parents? With God?

- Is there a way for them to repair the damage? What would you do?

What Is Sin?

God and the Church tell us that certain behaviors are sinful because they disrupt or destroy our growth as human and as spiritual beings. When we intentionally do what we know is wrong, we lose respect for ourselves. We lose faith in ourselves. Our self-esteem suffers because we see ourselves as less valuable or less worthy. Our sins also do real and lasting damage to our relationships with others and with God. The earliest Christians understood sin as "missing the mark." In other words, we miss our potential by certain actions, words, or thoughts.

God values us no matter what we do. The Bible tells us time and again how Jesus cares deeply for his lost sheep. Yet when we act in ways that hurt others or degrade ourselves, it's more difficult for us to love ourselves, love others, and love God. It is also more difficult for us to accept love from God and others.

When we can't accept the love that God and others offer us, we shut ourselves off from our spiritual nourishment. In this state, we are in great need of **reconciliation**, being brought back into harmony with God, others, and ourselves.

"Reconciliation with God is thus the purpose and the effect of the sacrament. For those who receive the sacrament of Penance with contrite heart and religious disposition, reconciliation 'is usually followed by peace and serenity of conscience with strong spiritual consolation.'"

CCC 1468

How Did Jesus Feel About Sin?

Reconciliation involves a change of heart, the forgiveness of sin, and the rebuilding of relationships. It was important in the ministry of Jesus, who constantly called people to repentance and heartfelt, sincere sorrow for wrongdoing. He tells us, "I did not come to call the righteous but sinners" (Matthew 9:13).

The ministry of Jesus made it clear that God's healing and mercy are communicated in very visible, human ways. Take a moment to read the story of the Prodigal Son (Luke 15:11–24). Keep in mind that at the time of Jesus, it was undignified and almost unheard of for a grown man to run; yet the father sprints across his fields to embrace his son.

The early Christian community believed Jesus had given the apostles and their successors the power to forgive sins. "He breathed on them and said to them, 'Receive the holy Spirit. Whose sins you forgive are forgiven them, and whose sins you retain are retained'" (John 20:22–23).

In the early Church, reconciliation took place through participation in the Eucharist (see Matthew 26:28), the anointing of the sick (see James 5:14–15), works of charity and fasting (see Luke 7:47 and Matthew 6:16), and correcting each other out of love (see Matthew 18:15–20 and 2 Thessalonians 3:14–15).

- What does this story tell you about God's love for you?

- When did the Church begin the ministry of reconciliation?

Suggested responses include:

- Matthew 6:14–15
  If we forgive others, God will forgive us.

- Matthew 18:21–22
  We must forgive often and without limit.

- Matthew 26:28
  Jesus' blood was shed for our forgiveness.

- Luke 17:3–4
  We should forgive those who sin against us.

- 1 John 1:9
  If we acknowledge our sins, and repent of them, God will forgive us.

How Does the Church Practice Reconciliation Today?

While sin may be secret, it is never private. Nothing we do is hidden from God, nor is anything we do totally isolated from others.

• How do our decisions impact those who care about us?

The purpose of the sacrament of reconciliation is to restore our relationship with God and our neighbor through God's forgiveness of our sins. It should help us celebrate our efforts to be a people of mercy and forgiveness. As Christians, we are called to be a people of reconciliation even if those actions are sometimes countercultural. As Christians, we are called to be God's instruments in removing the barriers that keep individuals and groups from communicating with and caring for each other.

When we participate in this sacrament, we must accept God's forgiveness and be willing to forgive others. When we have real sorrow for our sins, we want to do **penance** for them, to make up for whatever harm we have done. Doing penance helps bring about reconciliation.

The Church emphasizes that this sacrament, like all sacraments, belongs to the faith community. When we are healed as individuals, the entire body of Christ is strengthened.

"Sin damages or even breaks fraternal communion. The sacrament of Penance repairs or restores it. In this sense, it does not simply heal the one restored to ecclesial communion, but has also a revitalizing effect on the life of the Church which suffered from the sin of one of her members."

CCC 1469

How Do We Make the Most of This Sacrament?

As with all sacraments, there is nothing magical or automatic about what occurs. Poor or insincere preparation will result in an unsatisfying experience.

Good preparation begins with a good **examination of conscience**, a careful, honest look at ourselves and our behavior. It isn't to count up our good and bad deeds but to reflect on how well we have loved God, others, and ourselves. When examining our consciences, we shouldn't dwell on what we have done wrong but focus on what we failed to do or refused to do right. Not all sin is doing something wrong; sometimes a sin can be choosing not to act at all.

When we feel bad about our behavior, sharing those feelings with someone we trust can be a healing experience. When we name and face our sinful actions and habits, they lose much of their power over us. Facing sin and taking responsibility for actions that have hurt us or others are the first steps in healing. Listening to someone who will help guide us in the right direction is another important step.

Why Should I Tell My Sins to a Priest?

Just as a priest is Christ's representative during baptism, he is also Christ's representative in the sacrament of reconciliation. This ministry has been passed down from Christ to the apostles, and from the apostles to bishops and priests, for the sake of the Church community. The Catholic Church asks its members to confess their sins to a priest because it believes that sin, however secret, in some way hurts the growth and life of the community, as well as that of the sinner.

Because sin wounds the community, true reconciliation must include the community and not just God. In the confessional, the priest represents the whole Christ—the head who is Jesus and his body, the Church.

The penance that the priest gives us following confession should help us reflect seriously on what we can do to avoid sinful behavior and walk more closely with Jesus. Ideally, acts of penance given by the priest should be related to the sins committed. For example, if you have difficulty controlling your temper, your penance might be to practice patience. Once penance is given, the priest prays the prayer of reconciliation, also called **absolution**. At this time, our sins are forgiven by God through the priest.

How Does the Church Practice Reconciliation Today?

• Discuss how our decisions impact more than just us. Ask participants to share examples of this from their own lives.

Why Should I Tell My Sins to a Priest?

• Discuss the difference between penance and absolution. Ask participants why we need both absolution from the priest and to perform our penance joyfully.

Suggested responses include: Absolution is when God, through the priest, forgives our sins, but we can't be truly forgiven if we aren't truly sorry. A penance is an act that shows we repent our sins and genuinely want to try and do better.

• After reading how the Church practices reconciliation, talk about why the sacrament of reconciliation, like all the sacraments, belongs to the faith community and not to just the individual and God.

Suggested responses for the chart appear below.

CATECHUMENATE

JOURNEY OF FAITH

How the Sacrament Is Celebrated

1. Enter the **confessional**, a small room or space where the priest is seated.

2. Say, "Bless me, Father, for I have sinned." Then tell the priest that it's your first confession (or how long it's been since your last confession).

3. Name any sins you are sorry for and want to confess. Don't worry about listing each one in detail. Just explain how you disobeyed God and why you feel sad or apart from his love.

4. The priest will give you some advice. Listen carefully. He will then give you a penance. Penance is not punishment; it is a simple act you can do to make up for any hurt or damage your sins caused. Your penance will also help you grow closer to God and others.

5. Say an Act of Contrition prayer. Your leader can give you a copy.

6. The priest will pray over you and, with a sign of the cross, you are absolved (pardoned), by God through the priest.

7. Thank the priest as you leave, and remember to do your penance.

As a group, work on the chart below:

Sin	How does it hurt you?	How does it hurt others?	What might a penance be?
Gossiping			
Cheating			
Using God's name in vain			
Stealing			
Lying			
Bullying			

Recall a time when you were dishonest or hurt someone because you acted selfishly.

How did you feel when you realized what you'd done? Did you do anything to say you were sorry? If not, is there anything you could do now?

Journey of Faith for Teens: Catechumenate. C6 (826290)
Imprimi Potest: Stephen T. Rehrauer, CSsR, Provincial, Denver Province, the Redemptorists.
Imprimatur: "In accordance with CIC 827, permission to publish has been granted on March 23, 2016, by the Most Reverend Edward M. Rice, Auxiliary Bishop, Archdiocese of St. Louis. Permission to publish is an indication that nothing contrary to Church teaching is contained in this work. It does not imply any endorsement of the opinions expressed in the publication, nor is any liability assumed by this permission."
Journey of Faith © 2000, 2016 Liguori Publications, Liguori, MO 63057. To order, visit Liguori.org or call 800-325-9521 Liguori Publications, a nonprofit corporation, is an apostolate of the Redemptorists. To learn more about the Redemptorists, visit Redemptorists.com. All rights reserved. No part of this publication may be reproduced, distributed, stored, transmitted, or posted in any form by any means without prior written permission.
Text: Adapted from *Journey of Faith* © 2000 Liguori Publications. Editors of 2016 *Journey of Faith:* Theresa Nienaber and Pat Fosarelli, MD, DMin. Design: Lorena Mitre Jimenez. Images: Shutterstock. Unless noted, Scripture texts in this work are taken from *New American Bible,* revised edition © 2010, 1991, 1986, 1970 Confraternity of Christian Doctrine, Washington, D.C., and are used by permission of the copyright owner. All Rights Reserved. No part of New American Bible may be reproduced in any form without permission in writing from the copyright owner. Excerpts from English translation of the *Catechism of the Catholic Church* for the United States of America © 1994 United States Catholic Conference, Inc. —*Libreria Editrice Vaticana,* English translation of the *Catechism of the Catholic Church: Modifications from the Editio Typica* © 1997 United States Catholic Conference, Inc. —*Libreria Editrice Vaticana.* Compliant with *The Roman Missal, Third Edition.*
Printed in the United States of America. 20 19 18 17 16 / 5 4 3 2 1. Third Edition.

Liguori PUBLICATIONS
A Redemptorist Ministry

Sin	How does it hurt you?	How does it hurt others?	What might a penance be?
Gossiping	*Distances you from God and breaks trust with others...*	*Can ruin reputations, builds distrust, can ruin friendships...*	*To ask the person's forgiveness, to actively try to spread positive news...*
Cheating	*Keeps you from learning, builds distrust if you're caught...*	*Builds distrust...*	*To acknowledge what you did to the person(s) involved...*
Using God's name in vain	*Distances you from God...*	*Portrays your faith in a negative way...*	*To ask God's forgiveness and raise God's name up in prayers of praise...*
Stealing	*Separates you from the community...*	*Causes financial loss...*	*Return what was stolen and ask for forgiveness...*
Lying	*Breaks friendships or relationships, causes guilt or fear of being found out...*	*Builds relationships on false ground, builds distrust...*	*Ask for forgiveness and actively try to speak only the truth...*
Bullying	*Makes you less like Christ, distances you from God and others...*	*Can cause physical or emotional harm...*	*Ask for forgiveness, spread random acts of kindness, try to come to that person's defense in the future...*

Journaling

Recall a time when you were dishonest or hurt someone because you acted selfishly. How did you feel when you'd realized what you'd done? Did you do anything to say you were sorry? If not, is there anything you could do now?

Closing Prayer

As a closing prayer, have participants ask for the grace to improve one area of their lives. After a moment of silence for personal intentions, lead the group to respond, "Lord, hear our prayer."

Looking Ahead

Today's lesson looked at the sacramental life of the Church through healing and restoration. As participants prepare for the next lesson, ask them to consider how these graces of healing and restoration could provide strength during physical, as well as spiritual, struggles.

C7: The Sacrament of Anointing of the Sick

Catechism: 1499–1532

Objectives

- Identify instances from Jesus' healing ministry that led to the institution of the sacrament.
- Outline the basic steps in the sacrament.
- Describe the nature of the sacrament as going beyond "last rites" or preparation for death.

Leader Meditation

James 5:13–16

The early Church saw a great connection between the healing of the body and the healing of the soul. In this lesson, the participants will be asked to make a distinction between curing and healing. Reflect on this sacrament's emphasis on restored spiritual and emotional health.

Leader Preparation

- Read the lesson, this lesson plan, the Scripture passage, and the *Catechism* sections.
- If you can, display the blessed oil used in the anointing of the sick.

Welcome

Greet the group as it gathers. Check for supplies and immediate needs. Solicit questions or comments about the previous session and/or share new information and findings. Begin promptly.

Opening Scripture

James 5:13–16

Ask a volunteer to light the candle and read aloud. Explain that the sacred oil on the table was blessed by a bishop and is an important symbol connected with this sacrament. As the reading reveals, the sacred oil has its roots in the early Church. Before beginning your discussion of the lesson handout, ask participants: ***Does this reading have any similarities with reconciliation and penance? How might physical and spiritual healing be connected?***

> By the sacred anointing of the sick and the prayer of the priests the whole Church commends those who are ill to the suffering and glorified Lord, that he may raise them up and save them.
>
> *CCC 1499*

In Short:

- Anointing stems from Jesus' healing ministry.
- The sacrament follows basic steps.
- The sacrament is more than "last rites" or preparation for death.

The Sacrament of Anointing of the Sick

When Diane found out from her pastor, Fr. Joe, that her parish was going to offer the sacrament of the anointing of the sick during one of its Sunday Masses, she felt hopeful for the first time in weeks. Her mother had been battling cancer for more than a year, and the difficult chemotherapy treatments hadn't done much.

As she watched her mother suffer, Diane went through periods of doubting God's love and even God's existence. Yet she clung to her faith with the hope that it would somehow see her through these sorrow-filled days.

Diane was with her mother for the Sunday liturgy and the anointing. Her mother was also eager to receive the sacrament. But before the anointing, Fr. Joe wanted to share something important with the rest of the assembly.

He told the assembly that the sacrament of the anointing of the sick was not as much about curing as it was about healing. Curing a person deals with conquering the disease and repairing the body;

healing involves breathing life and hope into the person's spirit. While it's important to continually pray for a cure, spiritual healing is more connected to a person's joy and inner peace. Healing gives a person power over disease, sickness, and even death.

At first, Diane was disappointed. She wanted her mother cured! But in the weeks following the anointing, Diane began to understand.

She and her mother focused less on the disease and more on their relationship. They felt free to share and to pray in ways they never could before. They began to feel at peace in a way they never had. Many times, in the months before her mother's death, Diane felt a special closeness with her mother, and her mother felt at peace with her illness. Diane thought to herself, *This could only be the work of the Spirit.*

Physical and Spiritual Health

"Illness and suffering have always been among the gravest problems confronted in human life. In illness, man experiences his powerlessness, his limitations, and his finitude....It can also make a person more mature, helping him discern in his life what is not essential so that he can turn toward that which is."

CCC 1500–1501

People during Jesus' time saw a close relationship between soul and body. Jesus shared this attitude toward health and sickness. He was just as concerned with people's physical health as their spiritual health. In fact, the word *salvation* comes from the Latin word *salus*, which means "health."

CCC 1499–1532

The Sacrament of Anointing of the Sick

- Read the introductory story out loud together and give participants a chance to respond. Remind participants it is OK to feel disappointed, hurt, even angry for a time if a loved one gets sick and doesn't get better.

- Emphasize why *healing* is important and point out it is not just the sick person [Diane's mother] but the loved ones [Diane] who receive spiritual healing, too.

- Ask participants if they can think of examples of both curing and healing. Clarify any misunderstandings. (Curing would be anytime someone is miraculously cured of their illness. Healing is a change in attitude that makes us more at peace with our situation.)

Physical and Spiritual Health

- Discuss how our physical and spiritual health are connected. Ask participants to share any connections between their physical and spiritual health (stress, illness, and so on). Discuss how having a strong faith could make physical struggles easier to manage.

Jesus Shares His Healing Ministry

- If you have time, read the Scripture passages in the sidebar as a group and discuss what we can learn from these examples of Jesus' healing ministry.

Suggested responses include:

- Matthew 9:20–22
  Jesus says the woman is healed because of her faith.

- Mark 2:8–12
  Jesus heals physical and spiritual wounds (he physically heals the paralytic and forgives his sins). If you discuss this as a group, emphasize that this passage illustrates how Jesus heals all our wounds and not that physical illnesses or disabilities are the result of someone's sin.

- Luke 17:12–16
  Jesus heals us so that we can give praise and glory back to God for our healing.

- John 9:6–11
  Jesus heals us through our faith when we obey his commands.

In announcing the good news of salvation, Jesus was declaring that God cares not only for our souls but for our bodies as well. By healing people's bodies as well as their souls, Jesus showed that the entire human being is touched by God's salvation.

Jesus often cured people's physical ailments as a symbol of the spiritual healing taking place within their hearts. The ancient world seemed to know what scientists are now rediscovering—physical and spiritual well-being are closely connected.

> - Have you discovered a connection between your physical and spiritual health? What is it?
> - Do you think having strong faith makes physical struggles easier? Why or why not?

Jesus Shares His Healing Ministry

The Gospel makes it clear that Jesus shared his healing ministry with his apostles: "They drove out many demons, and they anointed with oil many who were sick and cured them" (Mark 6:13).

James 5:14–15 tells us, "Is anyone among you sick? He should summon the presbyters of the church, and they should pray over him and anoint [him] with oil in the name of the Lord, and the prayer of faith will save the sick person, and the Lord will raise him up. If he has committed any sins, he will be forgiven." This Scripture passage tells us that the healing ministry was very much active and alive in the early Church. Again, we hear of the powerful connection between the human body and the human spirit. We also learn the importance of knowing that our sins are forgiven, especially in the face of serious illness or death. Freedom from the destructive power of sin is, in itself, a tremendously healing force.

> Read these instances of Jesus healing. What stands out to you? What do they tell you about his healing ministry?
>
> Matthew 9:20–22   Mark 2:8–12
>
> Luke 17:12–16   John 9:6–11

How Is the Anointing of the Sick Celebrated Today?

"This sacred anointing of the sick was instituted by Christ our Lord as a true and proper sacrament of the New Testament. It is alluded to indeed by Mark, but is recommended to the faithful and promulgated by James the apostle and brother of the Lord."

CCC 1511

The rite of this sacrament (the words and actions that accompany the sacrament) begins with a Liturgy of the Word so that those who have gathered may be strengthened and instructed by specially chosen Scripture passages.

Next is the laying on of hands, an ancient Christian gesture. In both the Old Testament and the New Testament, the laying on of hands symbolizes and grants the giving of the special grace of the Holy Spirit. In this way, the sick are singled out for the Spirit's special care. In today's rite, the celebrant silently lays his hands upon the heads of those to be anointed.

Then the blessing of the oil is given. Oil is a powerful biblical symbol. In the ancient world, it was used by athletes before competition. Oil was also the fuel that gave people light for their homes, and oil lamps burned continually in the Jerusalem Temple. In the desert, oil brought relief against the drying winds.

Oil, a symbol of the penetrating presence of the Holy Spirit, helps us to understand what is happening during the anointing of the sick. Oil is rubbed and absorbed into the skin just like the Holy Spirit enters the sick person to help him or her be more aware of and open to the healing power of God.

How Is the Anointing of the Sick Celebrated Today?

- In groups, have participants create a list (or visual) of the steps of anointing of the sick. If you're short on time, create a written list as a group. If you have plenty of time, encourage participants to be creative and create a list, comic book-style panels, a story, and so on.

Suggested responses include:

1. Begins with the Liturgy of the Word.

2. The laying on of hands.

3. The blessing of the oil.

4. The anointing (a sign of the cross is traced in oil on the head and oil is rubbed into the hands).

5. The priest says, "May the Lord who frees you from sin save you and raise you up."

Next is the actual anointing in which the sign of the cross is traced with oil on the head and oil is rubbed into the hands. The cross is the mark of Christ, a sign that we belong to him. Whether our particular sickness involves physical pain, emotional pain, or spiritual suffering, Christ the healer comes to us in our own special circumstances.

As the priest anoints the person with the precious oil, he says: "May the Lord who frees you from sin save you and raise you up."

What Can Someone Expect From This Sacrament?

The anointing of the sick does not promise a miraculous physical cure; however, we are assured of healing in the ways that are most important. In other words, we can expect that God will give us exactly what we need at that moment (not necessarily what we want at the time) to assure our salvation and our greater peace with God.

As with all the sacraments, people must be sincere in their faith and come to the sacrament with an open mind and heart. Whether they desire mental and emotional healing and strength, an actual cure from a serious sickness or disease, or the grace to courageously face the last hours of their lives, God's response is always real and complete—not just to the body, not just to the spirit, but to the whole human person.

Not long ago, the anointing of the sick was called *extreme unction* (meaning "last anointing"). It was only for those close to death. When a priest was called to give the last rites, it was because that person was not expected to live much longer. But as we have already seen, the sacrament was not originally intended to be that way.

The Second Vatican Council helped to bring this sacrament back to its original purpose. The council changed *extreme unction* to *anointing of the sick*. It also said the sacrament is for anyone suffering from an illness. Dying people receive the sacraments of reconciliation and Eucharist at the same time they receive anointing of the sick. In this situation, prayers used in the anointing of the sick are changed slightly to ask more for spiritual strength than physical healing.

Priests are the only ones who can administer the sacrament of the anointing of the sick. However, healing ministry to the sick is a responsibility of the entire Christian community, not just the priest. If we are to follow in the footsteps of Jesus, we must keep in mind that much of his work on earth was taking care of the weak, the poor, the hungry, and the sick.

Family and friends can do a lot to meet the spiritual needs of loved ones who are sick. The spiritual needs of the sick may include forgiveness for wrongdoing, the need to resolve conflicts, the need to know they are cared for, the need to know that they are loved despite any disabilities, and the need to know that they will not be abandoned in their final hours. We are all challenged to do everything we can to reach out to those who are suffering, just as Jesus and his followers did.

- *Even though only a priest can administer the sacrament, why is it important for the whole community to participate in healing ministry?*
- *What are some ways you can participate?*

What Can Someone Expect From This Sacrament?

- Emphasize that while only a priest can administer the sacrament, everyone is involved in Jesus' healing ministry.

- Discuss why community is important to the healing ministry.

Suggested responses include: If we're going to live like Jesus we need to provide comfort to the sick, by taking care of others we can be Christ's hands in the world, by offering our presence to others we can heal them of loneliness and isolation, and more.

Answers to the lesson activity appear below.

(1) *healing*

(2) *laying on of hands*

(3) *penetrating*

(4) *sign of the cross*

(5) *oil*

(6) *"May the Lord who frees you from sin save you and raise you up."*

Journey of Faith for Teens: Catechumenate, C7 (826290)
Imprimi Potest: Stephen T. Rehrauer, CSsR, Provincial, Denver Province, the Redemptorists.
Imprimatur: "In accordance with CIC 827, permission to publish has been granted on March 23, 2016, by the Most Reverend Edward M. Rice, Auxiliary Bishop, Archdiocese of St. Louis. Permission to publish is an indication that nothing contrary to Church teaching is contained in this work. It does not imply any endorsement of the opinions expressed in the publication; nor is any liability assumed by this permission."
Journey of Faith © 2000, 2016 Liguori Publications, Liguori, MO 63057. To order, visit Liguori.org or call 800-325-9521. Liguori Publications, a nonprofit corporation, is an apostolate of the Redemptorists. To learn more about the Redemptorists, visit Redemptorists.com. All rights reserved. No part of this publication may be reproduced, distributed, stored, transmitted, or posted in any form by any means without prior written permission.
Text: Adapted from *Journey of Faith* © 2000 Liguori Publications. Editors of 2016 *Journey of Faith*: Theresa Nienaber and Pat Fosarelli, MD, DMin. Design: Lorena Mitre Jimenez. Images: Shutterstock. Unless noted, Scripture texts in this work are taken from *New American Bible*, revised edition © 2010, 1991, 1986, 1970 Confraternity of Christian Doctrine, Washington, D.C., and are used by permission of the copyright owner. All Rights Reserved. No part of *New American Bible* may be reproduced in any form without permission in writing from the copyright owner. Excerpts from English translation of the *Catechism of the Catholic Church* for the United States of America © 1994 United States Catholic Conference, Inc. —Libreria Editrice Vaticana. English translation of the *Catechism of the Catholic Church: Modifications from the Editio Typica* © 1997 United States Catholic Conference, Inc. —Libreria Editrice Vaticana. Compliant with *The Roman Missal, Third Edition.*
Printed in the United States of America. 20 19 18 17 16 / 5 4 3 2 1. Third Edition.

Liguori
PUBLICATIONS
A Redemptorist Ministry

Journal Prompt

Keeping in mind that sickness comes in many forms, think of someone who is in need of healing. What are some simple, practical ways you can be the healing hands of God for that person?

Closing Prayer

As a closing prayer, ask each participant to silently reflect on someone he or she knows who is in need of healing, physical or spiritual. Spend a moment or two in quiet reflection and then allow time for participants to mention their intention out loud. Pray the Our Father as a group.

Take-home

While the sacraments that have already been discussed are participated in by an individual and involve great interior reflection, there is still a strong and necessary community element. Before the next lesson, ask participants to think about why community is so important to fully experiencing the sacraments.

C8: The Sacrament of Matrimony

Catechism: 1533–1535, 1601–1666

Objectives

- Identify ways sacramental marriage reflects both Christ's paschal mystery and the love of the Trinity.
- Define marriage as self-giving, forgiving, faithful, indissoluble, intimate, unifying, and (pro) creative.
- Recall Catholic teaching on annulments and nontraditional unions.

Leader Meditation

Colossians 3:12–17

How does this passage encourage us to treat one another? Consider not only spouses but friends, coworkers, neighbors, and more. Consider your own attitudes toward marriage and the blessings, as well as difficulties, you may have encountered in relationships.

Leader Preparation

- Read the lesson, this lesson plan, the Scripture passage, and the *Catechism* sections. As you read this lesson, be particularly sensitive to the feelings of participants who may have parents who are recently divorced, separated, or remarried.

Welcome

Greet participants as they arrive. Check for supplies and immediate needs. Solicit questions or comments about the previous session and/or share new information and findings. Begin promptly.

Opening Scripture

Colossians 3:12–17

Ask for a volunteer to come to the table, light the candle, and read aloud. Before beginning your discussion of the lesson handout, ask participants: **How are the traits listed in this reading (compassion, humility, forgiveness…) necessary to building and maintaining healthy relationships?**

> The matrimonial covenant, by which a man and a woman establish between themselves a partnership of the whole of life,…has been raised by Christ the Lord to the dignity of a sacrament. *CCC 1601*

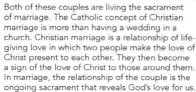

In Short:

- Marriage reflects the paschal mystery.
- Marriage reflects the love of the Trinity.
- Marriage has many spiritual characteristics.

The Sacrament of Matrimony

Melanie would never admit it, but she was a little jealous of her sister Kim. Kim and her boyfriend, Michael, had just gotten married. Even after their first year of marriage, Kim and Mike still acted like they had when they started dating. They loved doing things together and were always there to support each other. When Melanie asked her sister how she knew Mike was the right person to marry, Kim said it was because he was her best friend, her partner for the good and bad times.

Antoine's grandparents had been married for over fifty-two years. The past few years had been the hardest, though. Antoine's grandfather was starting to forget things and couldn't take care of himself anymore. But the way Antoine's grandma treated him never changed. "I loved him then and I love him now," she always said. Antoine wondered if he could ever do that, give himself to someone else completely and selflessly for love.

- What do these stories tell you about marriage?
- What does love mean to you?

Both of these couples are living the sacrament of marriage. The Catholic concept of Christian marriage is more than having a wedding in a church. Christian marriage is a relationship of life-giving love in which two people make the love of Christ present to each other. They then become a sign of the love of Christ to those around them. In marriage, the relationship of the couple is the ongoing sacrament that reveals God's love for us.

"The entire Christian life bears the mark of the spousal love of Christ and the Church…. Since it signifies and communicates grace, marriage between baptized persons is a true sacrament of the New Covenant."

CCC 1617

What Did Jesus Have to Say About Marriage?

"Husbands, love your wives, even as Christ loved the church and handed himself over for her."

Ephesians 5:25

Jesus showed us God's design for marriage in many ways. He was born into a human family, a sign of the importance and holiness of ordinary family life (Luke 2). He worked his first miracle at the wedding feast of Cana (John 2:1–11), an indication that the love of husband and wife are to be celebrated. He taught that married love must be faithful (Matthew 5:27–28). He proclaimed that true married love was meant to last forever (Mark 10:6–9).

CCC 1533–1535, 1601–1666

The Sacrament of Matrimony

- Discuss the opening anecdotes. Give participants time to talk about what love means to them. Allow them to share personal stories if they feel comfortable. Be prepared to share what love means to you.

What Did Jesus Have to Say About Marriage?

- Go over the Scripture passages listed. As you do, emphasize how the sacrament has its roots in both Church tradition and the Bible.

Suggested responses include:

- Luke 2:41–52
  While not about marriage itself, the finding of Jesus in the Temple shows how Jesus lived as part of a family and obeyed his parents, and how Mary and Joseph, as a married couple, looked out for their Son.

- John 2:1–12
  The wedding at Cana is the site of Jesus' first miracle and the beginning of his public ministry. The fact that he chose a wedding as the place to perform his first public miracle shows in what high regard Jesus held marriage.

- Matthew 5:27–30
  Here Jesus teaches about purity of heart and the responsibility we have to look at others with love and respect. Jesus even goes so far as to say looking at another with lust is adultery of the heart.

- Mark 10:6–9
  This teaching explains that a sacramental marriage is meant to be between one man and one woman who will become "one flesh." Jesus also teaches that "no human being must separate" this sacramental bond.

- Ephesians 5:22–30
  This passage isn't about women being lesser than men, rather it describes the mutual sacrifice required in marriage. A husband and wife must give of themselves to each other, expecting nothing in return just as Christ loved the Church enough to die for our sins.

What Does the Church Teach About Marriage?

- Discuss why marriage is such an important sacrament in the Church.

Suggested responses include: Marriage becomes a sign of Christ's love for his people; marriage is a vocation that brings the couple closer to Christ through sacrifice, forgiveness, and faithfulness; marriage is the foundation of family life and the domestic church.

- Emphasize the connection between the love of husband and wife and the love of God for the Church.

- If you have time, you may want to read paragraph 1604 in the *Catechism* stressing the line, "Since God created him man and woman, their mutual love becomes an image of the absolute and unfailing love with which God loves man."

- You may also want to return to the Scripture passage from Ephesians 5:22–30 you discussed above, stressing verse 25, "Husbands, love your wives, even as Christ loved the church and handed himself over for her."

Pick one or two of the following Scripture stories to read and write or discuss what it teaches about marriage.

Luke 2:41–52   John 2:1–12

Matthew 5:27–30   Mark 10:6–9

Ephesians 5:22–30

What Does the Church Teach About Marriage?

Marriage wasn't invented by the Church, but was authored by God from the beginning of time. Jesus presented the idea of marriage as sacrament through his ministry. In fact, the first miracle Jesus performed was turning water into wine at a wedding (John 2:1–12). This act is more than just the beginning of Jesus' public ministry, it is "confirmation of the goodness of marriage and the proclamation that thenceforth marriage will be an efficacious sign of Christ's presence" (CCC 1613).

The way we celebrate weddings has changed through the centuries, but the foundation of the sacrament of marriage remains the same. When Jesus said, "what God has joined together, no human being must separate" (Matthew 19:6), he meant a sacramental marriage forms an indissoluble bond (CCC 1615) that reflects the indissoluble bond between Jesus and the Church.

> "Jesus himself gives the strength and grace to live marriage in the new dimension of the Reign of God. It is by following Christ...that spouses will be able to 'receive' the original meaning of marriage and live it with the help of Christ."
>
> CCC 1615

To live marriage as a sacrament means that husband and wife become a sign of Christ's love for each other and for all the people who touch their lives. All relationships encounter hardships. Over the weeks, months, and years of a marriage, there are many opportunities for learning to accept, to be tolerant, and—especially—to forgive. This is why it's important to know the difference between romance and the love that forms the foundation of marriage. We may not always feel in love with someone, but marriage asks spouses to continuously choose to love each other.

When married couples remain faithful to their love for each other through times of difficulty and pain, they become closer to Christ and show something of Christ's ever-faithful love to others. This is why we say that marriage is an ongoing sacrament. To further emphasize the importance of this relationship, the husband and wife perform as ministers of this sacrament. The priest stands as a witness.

Are Protestant Marriages Sacramental?

When we say something is sacramental, we mean that it is a sign of Christ. The Catholic Church believes that a marriage between two baptized Christians is sacramental, a sign of Christ's love alive in our world, even if they were not married in a Catholic Church. The Church also teaches that a marriage between two Protestants cannot be broken by divorce any more than a marriage between two Catholics, because both unions are considered sacred and sacramental.

> - Why do you think the relationship between a married couple is so important to the life of the Church?

What Is Love?

> "If I give away everything I own, and if I hand my body over so that I may boast but do not have love, I gain nothing."
>
> 1 Corinthians 13:3

Love is self-giving. God is the ultimate giver. God gave us the most precious gift a loving parent could give—God's beloved Son, Jesus. Because married love comes from God and is based on the nature of God, it is self-giving. Total loving means total giving.

When we love, we give of our joy, our interest, our understanding, our knowledge, and our time. We do not give up or sacrifice who we are, but we give who we are to the person we love. This is a more difficult task than it sounds. It takes a lot of courage to allow someone to see us for who we truly are, our faults and failings, as well as our gifts.

But this also means we are free to grow with another person. Just like good friends make you excited about new things or bring out your best self, so

---

What Is Love?

- Ask participants if their definition of love has changed from the beginning of the lesson.

- Discuss the difference between romance and the kind of love necessary for a marriage and as a group create a list of similarities and differences between the two.

Suggested responses include: romance is more emotional, romance can be fleeting—we don't feel romantic all the time, love is choosing to be faithful and forgiving, love means seeing the flaws in the other person and not just what attracts you, love

requires working for your spouse's salvation....

- Ask participants if how they think about God's love for them has changed. Discuss similarities and difference between the kind of love talked about in this lesson and God's love for us.

Suggested responses include: God's love for us is perfect but our love for each other can sometimes be flawed, God's love for us never wavers, just like God wants our salvation we want the best for the people we love....

does marriage shape who you are and who you will become. True love is a constant call to grow—to become more than we ever imagined we could be.

> "[Love] does not brood over injury, it does not rejoice over wrongdoing but rejoices with the truth."
>
> *1 Corinthians 13:5–6*

Love is forgiving. When you have a serious disagreement with your best friend, and then you talk about the problem and forgive one another, is your friendship stronger than ever? This is often the case with married love. Forgiveness and acceptance lead to growth and a stronger relationship.

God's endless, constant forgiveness of us is reflected in the way a couple talks about their differences, forgives hurts, and heals one another. The couple's willingness to heal their relationship and let go of personal gain is an example of the desire for reconciliation that God has for us.

> "[Love] bears all things, believes all things, hopes all things, endures all things."
>
> *1 Corinthians 13:7*

Love is faithful. A man and woman are asked on their wedding day, "Will you love and honor each other as husband and wife for the rest of your lives?" Wouldn't it be reasonable if they replied, "Yes, provided everything goes according to our plan?" But that's not the answer they give. They each reply, "I will."

Marriage, like all human relationships, rarely goes according to plan. Outside influences, such as job changes, illnesses, accidents, and aging parents often place unexpected stress on a married couple. The challenge of raising children is sometimes more difficult than the couple anticipated.

No spouse and no marriage are perfect. Real love is love that endures long after the honeymoon is over. During periods of hardship, real love is not something we feel. It is something we live. Often real love seems more like a commitment than a feeling. Feelings are fleeting and changeable. Faithful, committed love is constant.

God's faithfulness to people is evident in the commitment a couple makes to love each other for a lifetime. God's love is visible when a weary wife listens in the middle of the night because her husband needs to talk. It is visible when a spouse helps around the house even though he or she had plans to go out. God's faithfulness accepts us for who we are, affirms us, looks for the good in us, and challenges us to grow. A married couple should reflect God's love in how they affirm and challenge one another.

• Has your definition of love changed from the beginning of this lesson? How?

Love is intimate and creative. It is impossible for us to understand the mystery of the Holy Trinity and the oneness of God the Father, God the Son, and God the Holy Spirit. But it is possible to recognize the strength and beauty of a couple who is truly one in the sense that they are more complete, more perfect in their togetherness. In the blending of the two into one flesh, we, the Church, can catch a glimpse of the oneness of God.

Because the couple shares in God's creative love, they are privileged to share in the most exalted part of God's creative work—the creation of another human being. This particular creative act comes with the responsibility of raising the child in the faith and educating her or him by both examples and words.

Why Wait

You might be wondering why, if sex is such a meaningful and God-centered thing, the Church is always telling people they can't do it. While this is an attitude many Christians have shared, it's not quite right. The Church isn't saying, "NO!" It's saying, "Not yet...."

Because the Church sees sex as so meaningful (it's sharing in God's creative act!), it reserves sex for only the most permanent of relationships—a relationship that becomes the foundation of a family.

Why Wait?

• Ask participants what they think about the Church's teaching on abstaining from sex until marriage. If you have time, read *CCC* 2337 about chastity.

• Ask participants if there are other things they've waited for until a more appropriate time (getting a part-time job, going away to college, driving...).

What Do Catholics Believe About Divorce?

- As you discuss divorce and annulment, emphasize that this process isn't to figure out who was wrong or right. Give participants time to ask questions. If you don't know an answer, talk to your parish priest and respond next time.

With a partner or as a group, brainstorm some characteristics or traits of a Christian marriage. Then discuss how each of these traits reflects God's love for us.

Suggested responses include:

Traits of a Christian marriage: *God-centered, respectful, lifting each other up, open to life....*

How they reflect God: *focuses on the salvation of the other, is unconditional, is creative....*

What Do Catholics Believe About Divorce?

"The Church, after an examination of the situation by the competent ecclesiastical tribunal, can declare the nullity of marriage, [that is], that the marriage never existed. In this case the contracting parties are free to marry, provided the natural obligations of a previous union are discharged."

CCC 1629

Because the Church believes that marriage is a sacrament, a divorce can't dissolve it. The Church teaches that a marriage can be annulled, which means a sacramental marriage never happened in the first place. This doesn't mean everyone pretends the wedding didn't take place or that a family wasn't really formed (children whose parents received an annulment aren't considered illegitimate). By saying "the marriage never existed" the Church means the sacramentality of the marriage was never present. That means that even before the wedding took place, the couple was unable to give of themselves freely and completely.

The process of annulling a marriage isn't about blaming anyone for messing up the marriage. Actually, it's about healing two people who weren't whole when they came to the marriage initially.

With a partner or as a group, brainstorm some characteristics or traits of a Christian marriage. Then discuss how each of these traits reflects God's love for us.

In your own words, attempt to define and describe real love (it doesn't have to be romantic love!).

If you enjoy being creative, you may write a poem or compose a song.

Journey of Faith for Teens: Catechumenate, C8 (826290)
Imprimi Potest: Stephen T. Rehrauer, CSsR, Provincial, Denver Province, the Redemptorists.
Imprimatur: "In accordance with CIC 827, permission to publish has been granted on March 23, 2016, by the Most Reverend Edward M. Rice, Auxiliary Bishop, Archdiocese of St. Louis. Permission to publish is an indication that nothing contrary to Church teaching is contained in this work. It does not imply any endorsement of the opinions expressed in the publication, nor is any liability assumed by this permission."
Journey of Faith © 2000, 2016 Liguori Publications, Liguori, MO 63057. To order, visit Liguori.org or call 800-325-9521. Liguori Publications, a nonprofit corporation, is an apostolate of the Redemptorists. To learn more about the Redemptorists, visit Redemptorists.com. All rights reserved. No part of this publication may be reproduced, distributed, stored, transmitted, or posted in any form by any means without prior written permission.
Text: Adapted from *Journey of Faith* © 2000 Liguori Publications. Editors of 2016 *Journey of Faith*: Theresa Nienaber and Pat Fosarelli, MD, DMin. Design: Lorena Mitre Jimenez. Images: Shutterstock. Unless noted, Scripture texts in this work are taken from *New American Bible*, revised edition © 2010, 1991, 1986, 1970 Confraternity of Christian Doctrine, Washington, D.C., and are used by permission of the copyright owner. All Rights Reserved. No part of *New American Bible* may be reproduced in any form without permission in writing from the copyright owner. Excerpts from English translation of the *Catechism of the Catholic Church* for the United States of America © 1994 United States Catholic Conference, Inc. —Libreria Editrice Vaticana. English translation of the *Catechism of the Catholic Church: Modifications from the Editio Typica* © 1997 United States Catholic Conference, Inc. —Libreria Editrice Vaticana. Compliant with *The Roman Missal, Third Edition*. Printed in the United States of America. 20 19 18 17 16 / 5 4 3 2 1. Third Edition.

Liguori PUBLICATIONS
A Redemptorist Ministry

Journaling

In your own words, attempt to define and describe real love (it doesn't have to be romantic love!). If you enjoy being creative, you may write a poem or compose a song.

Closing Prayer

Ask participants to silently call to mind their parents and any other relationships that have helped them better understand the love of God. Then read 1 Corinthians 13:1–7 as a closing meditation.

Looking Ahead

Marriage builds a foundation for the family, also called the domestic church, but there are many people building the Church who aren't married. Before the next class, have participants think about their larger Church family and identify some people who are working to build that foundation.

Catechism: 1536–1600

Objectives

- Differentiate between the orders of deacon, priest, and bishop.
- Distinguish between the universal priesthood and the ordained priesthood.
- Recognize the roots of the sacrament described in Scripture and accounts of the early Church.
- Identify the conferring event as the laying on of hands.

Leader Meditation

Mark 10:43–45

Reflect on Jesus' message that to serve others is to serve God. As an RCIA leader, you are serving God by teaching the men and women under your guidance. Ask our Lord for the wisdom and grace to serve them well.

Leader Preparation

Read the lesson, this lesson plan, the Scripture passage, and the *Catechism* sections.

Find a musical rendition of "Here I Am, Lord" for the closing prayer (if you can't find a recording or can't play music in your room you can read the verse from Scripture, 1 Samuel 3:7–10, instead).

Be familiar with the vocabulary term for this lesson: celibacy. The definition is provided in this guide's glossary.

Welcome

Greet participants as they arrive. Check for supplies and immediate needs. Solicit questions or comments about the previous session and/or share new information and findings. Begin promptly.

Opening Scripture

Mark 10:43–45

Ask a volunteer to light the candle and read aloud. Discuss the powerful message that Jesus gave his apostles. Emphasize that service to others was not a mere suggestion—it was a command! We serve God best by serving God's people. Before beginning your discussion of the lesson handout, ask participants to think about **why Jesus called the leaders of his Church to service rather than power.**

> The sacrament of Holy Orders communicates a "sacred power" which is none other than that of Christ. The exercise of this authority must therefore be measured against the model of Christ, who by love made himself the least and servant of all.
>
> *CCC 1551*

Journey of Faith

- What about these three examples stands out to you?
- How do you witness to your faith?

The Sacrament of Holy Orders

As the early Church began to grow, the apostles were in need of assistants, so they chose men "filled with the Spirit and wisdom" to help them minister to the people. Among these first deacons was a man named Stephen. Many people "came forward and debated with Stephen, but they could not withstand the wisdom and the spirit with which he spoke." So these men began to plot against him, and Deacon Stephen was stoned to death for refusing to stop preaching the word of God (Acts 6:1–15).

A prisoner had escaped from a World War II concentration camp in Auschwitz. In retaliation, the Nazi commandant chose ten other prisoners to be starved to death. One of the chosen young men sobbed, "My wife, my children!" Fr. Maximilian Kolbe stepped forward. "I want to die in place of this prisoner," he said. The commandant snapped, "Request granted."

Tens of thousands of people journeyed to Philadelphia in September 2015 to see Pope Francis. Some waited outside in lines for hours just to catch a glimpse of the pontiff. Why? Some were looking for a special blessing, others wanted to be part of the historic event, and some needed inspiration to stay hopeful in a troubled world.

All three of the men above are powerful examples of living a vocation to the ordained priesthood. By becoming an ordained priest, these men became servants for Christ and the Church. But being a priest doesn't always mean making a radical, public show of faith. In fact, the most powerful thing a priest can do is live a life of humble service and sacrifice.

Did Christ Ordain Priests?

"Holy Orders is the sacrament through which the mission entrusted by Christ to his apostles continues to be exercised in the Church until the end of time."

CCC 1536

The foundation of the priesthood goes back to the Old Covenant. Among his Chosen People, God designated the tribe of Levi for liturgical services. The role of the Old Covenant priest was to "act on behalf of men in relation to God, to offer gifts and sacrifices for sins" (CCC 1539). This priesthood became perfected in Christ, who only needed to sacrifice himself once for all time (CCC 1545).

TEENS

CCC 1536–1600

C9

The Sacrament of Holy Orders

- After reading the introductory stories, ask participants what stands out to them about these men. Discuss what it means to be a witness to your faith and ask participants to share witness stories of their own.

Did Christ Ordain Priests?

- If time allows, read from Matthew 10, Mark 6:1–3, and John 20:23. Ask participants to identify ways Jesus calls and instructs his apostles.

Suggested responses include:

- Matthew 10
  Jesus gives his disciples authority over unclean spirits and to cure disease and illnesses and commands them to use these gifts without collecting any money. He also cautions them that not everyone will be open to their message of the good news.

- Mark 6:1–3
  Jesus teaches in the synagogue at Nazareth, but his own people don't believe his words. Jesus is not discouraged, and he continues to minister to the people who do believe in him and leaves the ones who will not listen.

- John 20:23
  Jesus gives his disciples the power to forgive sins.

- Discuss why Jesus left his apostles with instructions on how to lead the Church.

Suggested responses include: Jesus wanted to make sure the disciples continued his work when he was gone, Jesus wanted to lay a foundation for his Church and we can see the beginning of the sacraments in his work on earth, Jesus wanted to empower his disciples to continue his work so people knew their power and knowledge came from him....

Who Were the Priests of the Early Church?

- Ask participants to describe, in their own words, the difference between the universal and ordained priesthood.

Suggested responses include: The universal priesthood is what every baptized person is called to participate in; the ordained priesthood are those who follow in the footsteps of the disciples to teach, preach, and officially minister.

- Discuss what responsibilities go with each of these roles and emphasize *all* Catholics are members of the universal priesthood.

Suggested responses include:

The universal priesthood: *to use the graces we receive at baptism to live like Christ, to use our talents to serve others, to build up the Church and others, to forgive others, to be living examples of Christ in the world....*

The ordained priesthood: *to serve the faithful, to teach the word of God, to celebrate the Eucharist and the other sacraments, to guide those in the universal priesthood....*

Jesus then sent his disciples out to preach and baptize (see Matthew 10). They were given the power to heal (see Mark 6:1–3) and to forgive sins (see John 20:23). At the Last Supper, when our Lord instructed his friends to "do this in memory of me," he was giving them the power to celebrate the Eucharist.

While the expression of the sacrament of holy orders was not exactly the same as it is today, the essential elements of the sacramental reality remain consistent. The apostles did serve the Church as the first priests and bishops "in the name and in the person of Christ the Head in the midst of the community" (*CCC* 1591) and through the unbroken line of apostolic succession, the bishops and priests of today do the same. The Gospel also shows the laying on of hands as a key symbol in this ordination.

"The holy Spirit said, 'Set apart for me Barnabas and Saul for the work to which I have called them.' Then, completing their fasting and prayer, they laid hands on them and sent them off."

Acts 13:2–3

"I remind you to stir into flame the gift of God that you have through the imposition of my hands."

2 Timothy 1:6

- Why do you think Jesus gave specific instructions to those who would lead his Church?

Who Were the Priests of the Early Church?

Like the Church today, the early Church believed that all the baptized shared in the priesthood of Christ, also called the universal priesthood. As promised by Christ, the Holy Spirit filled the faithful with different gifts. The early Christians recognized and used these special gifts and abilities for building up the people of God, the priestly community. Saint Paul tells us that some believers could heal, work miracles, or prophesy. Others could speak in tongues or understand and interpret the Spirit. Some could preach or teach (see 1 Corinthians 12).

Those blessed with the ability to effectively preach and teach eventually became Church leaders. As leaders called by God, their position was set apart by the laying on of hands and the calling down of the Holy Spirit (see 2 Timothy 1:6–7). This marked the beginning of formal ordination, or the making of an official minister. While everyone could proclaim the word and witness to the faith, only the ordained leader had the power to preach in the assembly, to celebrate the Eucharist, and to guide the faith community.

We see this tradition continue today in the sacrament of holy orders. The bishops, standing as the apostles, confer, or hand on, this sacrament. Through the laying on of hands, the bishop passes down this role as servant to God's people. Additionally, the bishop asks the Holy Spirit to give the priest the grace he needs to lead and serve.

The Priest's Role

"The ministerial or hierarchical priesthood of bishops and priests, and the common priesthood of all the faithful participate, 'each in its own proper way, in the one priesthood of Christ.'"

CCC 1547

The priest's chief responsibilities are to bring about the presence of Christ in the Church and to share in Christ's role as teacher, leader, and sanctifier. A priest is chosen to act in the person of Christ. The sacrament of holy orders gives the priest the power to preach the Gospel, give service to his faith community, and celebrate Mass and the sacraments, just like the apostles.

The common or universal priesthood, Church members who are not ordained, also has an important role in the Church. All members of the laity have the task of spreading the good news and of being Christ for one another in their everyday lives. The responsibilities of the ordained priest and the layperson (as part of the universal priesthood) have quite a bit in common!

- As a group or with a partner, create a list of characteristics in a good priest.
- Which of these traits do you think are most important? Why?

The Priest's Role

- Have participants create a list of traits found in a good priest either on their own or in a group. Ask why they chose what they did and which they feel are most important.

Suggested responses include: listens, understands where people are coming from, is knowledgeable about the faith, trustworthy, willing to serve God's people, humble, respectful....

- If you have time and if your parish priest is available, ask him to come to your class and talk about what his duties to the parish are and how he lives his vocation.

What Are Holy Orders?

The sacrament of holy orders establishes bishops, priests, and deacons as official Church leaders. The emphasis in holy orders is not on powerful leadership but on faithful, dedicated service to the people of God.

Throughout history, the principal duty of the priest has been to offer sacrifice. In the Old Testament, the priest would offer sacrifice by killing an animal or burning a harvest offering so that the people could make up for their sins and be reconciled with God.

Christ came to offer a sacrifice, too, but he offered himself on the cross so that all of God's people might be reconciled with God. Christ was both offering and priest. There could be no greater sacrifice than that of our Lord offering himself totally to God through his death on the cross.

It remains the duty of today's priest to offer sacrifice. At Mass, the priest and the people offer themselves and are joined with the bread and wine that become the Body and Blood of our Lord. We all become one with Christ, the true priest.

The priest must also lead and teach his faith community. Jesus was always willing to seek out the lost, to care for the sick and injured in his flock, even to give his life to save them. In the ceremony of ordination, the men to be ordained are reminded to be like Christ the Good Shepherd, who came to serve rather than to be served.

> *"In the ecclesial service of the ordained minister, it is Christ himself who is present to his Church as Head of his Body, shepherd of his flock, high priest of the redemptive sacrifice, Teacher of Truth."*
>
> *CCC 1548*

Being like Christ is difficult work. Christ preached in words and parables that the people could apply to their daily lives. He showed mercy and forgiveness to sinners and never ran from the poor, sick, or disabled. He brought a message of physical and spiritual healing to all and stood by his people in their greatest need, even when they were weak, afraid, or unfaithful. Priests are called to do the same.

Because priests are human, they sometimes don't perform their duties perfectly. Jesus didn't expect us to be perfect, in fact, he expected weaknesses and failures to be part of his Church. Jesus knew the sufferings and trials of being human. But he also knew the joys and understanding of humanity, too. The same human nature that has at times brought great difficulties to the Church also allows priests to be more fully understanding of the struggles and temptations of this life.

- *Why might weakness and imperfections be necessary for a priest?*

- *How do your mistakes make you more understanding?*

Three Levels of Holy Orders

Most people associate holy orders with the priesthood, but priesthood is really the second of three levels of holy orders.

Deacon
A transitional deacon is a stage a seminarian goes through before becoming a priest. While not the same as a priest, a deacon can, with the permission of the bishop, preach, baptize, distribute the Eucharist, bring Communion to the sick, and officiate at marriages and funerals. He leads the people in prayer, reads Scripture, preaches, and teaches. A married man may be ordained a permanent deacon with the same duties, but if his wife dies, a permanent deacon cannot get remarried.

Priest
In the early Church, the bishops ministered to everyone. As the number of believers grew, the bishops were no longer able to care for all of them. Therefore, they ordained men to act in their place. These men were the first priests.

Priests have three important roles. First, they are called to preach by word and action. Second, they are the leaders of worship. Third, they are called to be leaders in the image of the Good Shepherd.

offering of the people he is called to present to God.

o Giving the book of Gospels (to deacons): a reminder of his mission to proclaim the Gospel of Christ.

Three Levels of Holy Orders

- Discuss with participants why Jesus would have called the leaders of his Church to service rather than power. Connect this to Jesus' own role as Savior who sacrificed himself rather than coming in worldly might and glory.

Suggested responses include: Jesus could have come in power but his mission was to serve; serving others reflects Jesus' own sacrifice for the Church....

What Are Holy Orders

- Discuss how imperfections and failures can make us more empathetic to others.

Suggested responses include: Jesus picked imperfect disciples because they can better understand where people are coming from; we become examples to others of how to use the grace of God to overcome our failures; imperfection keeps us humble because only God is perfect....

- If you have your list of traits handy, ask participants which of those traits have to do with understanding others.

- If you have time, you may also want to go over the symbols of holy orders (CCC 1574).

  o Laying on of hands: a reminder that this role and authority is passed down from Jesus through the disciples.

  o Anointing with holy chrism: a sign of the special anointing of the Holy Spirit.

  o Giving the book of the Gospels, rings, miter, and crosier (to bishops): a sign of his apostolic mission, his fidelity to the Church, and his office as shepherd.

  o Giving the paten and chalice (to priests): a reminder of the

Suggested responses to the
activity appear below.

	How are they the same?	How are they different?
Bishops and Priests	*Called to service, called to celibacy, authority comes from the disciples, celebrate the sacraments.*	*Bishops lead diocese and priests. Priests serve the people directly in parishes.*
Priests and Deacons	*Called to serve the people of a parish, called to proclaim the good news.*	*Priests celebrate the sacraments in their parish. Deacons assist the priest in service but cannot perform certain sacraments (like reconciliation or Eucharist).*
Priests and the Laity	*Called to service by God.*	*Priests are ordained to serve the laity. The laity can be called to nonordained religious life, marriage, or single life.*

Journaling

Catholics are called by God to a certain vocation (married life, priesthood/holy orders, and single or religious life). Spend some quiet time in prayer thinking about these choices. Is there one that seems to speak more strongly to you than the others? What about it seems appealing? Difficult?

Closing Prayer

After praying for any special intentions, ask the participants to sit in a comfortable position and reflect upon the words of 1 Samuel 3:7–10 either in song or spoken word.

Take-home

Bishops, priests, and deacons are called to serve the Church in specific ways, but we are all called to serve. In the spirit of Christ the servant, participants should perform some small act of service between now and your next meeting. Ask participants to reflect on how this act of service brings them closer to Christ and his Church.

C10: The People of God

Catechism: 56–64, 121–123, 128–130, 1961–1964

Objectives

- Recount major events in salvation history from Abraham to Jesus.
- Describe the connection between the Old and New Testaments and covenants.
- Identify Old Testament figures and the Israelites as our ancestors in faith.

Leader Meditation

Genesis 15—21, 24—46; Exodus 7—16

Throughout the Old Testament, we see God's constant presence with and protection of the people. We also see the people's constant struggle between faith and fear, between faithfulness to the Lord and the desire for earthly treasure. What do these Scripture passages tell you about God? About God's faithfulness? How do these passages connect you with God's people throughout history?

Leader Preparation

- Read the lesson, this lesson plan, the Scripture passage, and the *Catechism* sections.
- You should also familiarize yourself with the Old Testament stories this lesson covers: Abraham and Sarah, Joseph and the Pharaoh in Egypt, Moses leading the Israelites out of Egypt; Moses and the Ten Commandments, King David, King Solomon, the prophet John the Baptist.
- Be familiar with the vocabulary term for this lesson: covenant. The definition is provided in this guide's glossary.

Welcome

Greet participants as they arrive. Check for supplies and immediate needs. Solicit questions or comments about the previous session and/or share new information and findings. Begin promptly.

Opening Scripture

Genesis 15:1—6

Ask a volunteer to light the candle and read aloud. Reflect on God's promise of faithfulness. Before beginning your discussion of the lesson handout, ask participants to think about **how we know God walks faithfully beside us today.**

> God chose Abraham and made a covenant with him and his descendants. By the covenant God formed his people and revealed his law to them through Moses. Through the prophets, he prepared them to accept the salvation destined for all humanity.
>
> *CCC 72*

Journey of Faith

In Short:

- The Old and New Testaments record key events of our salvation history.
- The New Testament continues the Old Testament.
- We share a covenant with our ancestors in faith.

- Was your journey to God smooth or rough?
- Are there any obstacles in your way going forward?

The People of God

Your journey toward faith began the moment you became aware of God's presence in your life. Whether a powerful conversion experience or a gradual awakening, this awareness marked a starting point, the beginning of your active relationship with God.

This wasn't the start of God's relationship with you, though. There has never been a time when you were outside of God's awareness. You were fashioned in God's thought and brought to life by God's love. Your relationship is nothing new to God.

Your relationship with and experience of God is unique to you. But the experience of awakening to God and discovering his presence is common to all believers. The Old Testament tells the story of God's relationship with his people, the awakening of their awareness, and their flights from or journeys toward God. In these ancient stories, you may recognize your own. Seeking God and meaning in your life are journeys as old as humankind.

Beginning With Abraham

Genesis chapters 15—21

"The word of the LORD came to Abram in a vision: Do not fear, Abram! I am your shield, I will make your reward very great."

Genesis 15:1

After Adam and Eve, humanity wandered from God. After a while, only a few people who recognized God's presence in their lives were left. Among these few was a man called Abram.

God asked Abram to take his wife, Sarai, and go to a distant land. Leaving everything familiar behind and putting all their faith in God, they were led many miles to a land called Canaan. Here, God gave Abram and Sarai new names: Abraham, which means "father of many nations," and Sarah, which means "princess of the people." When God named someone, it meant that this person now belonged to God. Then God promised Abraham that his descendants would outnumber the stars in the sky and the sands of the earth. God's promise that Abraham would be the father of many nations is known as God's **covenant** (sacred promise) with Abraham or the old covenant.

CCC 56–64, 121–123, 128–130, 1961–1964

o Israel in a Foreign Land: *Isaac, the son of Abraham and Sarah, has a son Jacob. Jacob becomes the father of twelve, including Joseph. Joseph's brothers were jealous of him and sell him into slavery. Joseph uses God's gift of dream interpretation to help the Pharaoh and Egypt prepare for a great famine. Eventually Joseph is reunited with his brothers, forgives them, and saves them from starvation. Eventually all of Israel settles in Egypt.*

o Moses as Leader: *After years of peace, the new Pharaoh feels threatened by the Israelites and orders all newborn boys to be killed. Moses survives and is adopted by the Pharaoh's daughter. God appears to Moses in the burning bush. Moses is called to lead his people out of slavery and into freedom.*

o Slavery to Freedom: *Because the Pharaoh will not listen to Moses, God sends plagues onto the people of Egypt. Finally Moses is able to lead his people into freedom. However, the Israelites begin to turn away from God as they wander in the desert on their way to the Promised Land. It takes them forty years before they finally reach the Promised Land.*

The People of God

- Discuss the questions after the introductory text together. Be prepared to share your own triumphs and struggles getting to know God and building your faith. Encourage participants that the process of faith and conversion is never complete; we all grow, change, struggle, and try again.

- Rather than studying the rest of the lesson together, consider dividing participants into groups focusing on one of the next four sections. Groups should be responsible for: (1) reading the Scripture; (2) reading the lesson;

(3) identifying key people, events, and themes; (4) presenting their section to the group.

Suggested responses include:

o Beginning With Abraham: *After the Fall, humanity begins to lose its relationship with God. Abram and Sarai recognized God's presence in their lives. God called them to leave everything behind and follow him, which they did on faith. God gave them new names: Abraham and Sarah. God makes the old covenant (promise) to them that their descendants will outnumber the stars in the sky.*

Abraham and Sarah prospered in their new land and grew old, but they were childless. Still they trusted in God's promise of parenthood. When Sarah was very old, she finally gave birth to Isaac, whose name means "God's laugh."

The faith of Abraham and Sarah, their complete trust in God's plan, and the patience with which they waited for God's promise to be fulfilled led to their greatest joy, the miracle of Isaac.

- Have you ever had to leave something familiar (perhaps a school or neighborhood) and trust that God would be with you as you faced the unfamiliar?

Israel in a Foreign Land

Genesis chapters 37—45

"Jacob settled in the land where his father had sojourned, the land of Canaan."

Genesis 37:1

Isaac's son, Jacob, became the father of twelve sons. His second-youngest son, Joseph, was sold into slavery by his jealous brothers.

Joseph became a slave to Pharaoh in Egypt, but when Joseph helped Pharaoh interpret his troublesome dreams, Pharaoh rewarded Joseph by making him second in command.

Joseph's talent with dream interpretation helped him prepare Egypt for a terrible famine. During the famine, Joseph's brothers came to Egypt in search of food. His brothers bowed down before him when they realized that Joseph had saved Egypt (and his family) from starvation.

Joseph kissed his brothers and forgave them for their wicked act. Eventually the entire family of Israel lived in Egypt for many years with the blessing of Pharaoh.

- Like Joseph's brothers, have you ever learned something important from a mistake you made?

Moses as Leader

Exodus chapters 2—4

"A long time passed, during which the king of Egypt died. The Israelites groaned under their bondage and cried out....God heard their moaning and God was mindful of his covenant with Abraham, Isaac and Jacob."

Exodus 2:23–25

For a while, things went well for the Israelites in Egypt. As generations passed, the people experienced the kindness of God.

But a new Pharaoh felt threatened by the growing numbers of Israelite people and ordered soldiers to kill every newborn Israelite boy. One ingenious mother placed her baby son in a basket and hid him in the reeds by the river. Pharaoh's daughter found the baby and, though she knew he was an Israelite, disobeyed her father's command and adopted the baby, Moses. Moses' birth mother cleverly took a job as the baby's nurse so she could secretly teach him his heritage and his faith.

When Moses was grown, he left Egypt and lived as a simple shepherd. One day, while leading his sheep, Moses was struck by the sight of a burning bush. As he approached the bush, the voice of God commanded him to return to Egypt and tell Pharaoh to free his people.

Moses was frightened and wanted to refuse.

But God wouldn't let Moses off the hook. He gave Moses the power to perform miracles and allowed him to take his brother, Aaron, who was a good speaker.

- Has there ever been a time when you argued with God because you felt God asked too much of you?

Slavery to Freedom

Exodus, Deuteronomy

Moses' mission proved to be very difficult. When Moses and Aaron delivered God's command, Pharaoh laughed. So Egypt was struck by a series of disasters. But each time a plague would end, Pharaoh would break his promise to free God's people.

Then came the final and most terrible sign of all.

Moses told the Israelites to prepare their homes by smearing the blood of a lamb on their doorways. This would be a sign that they were a family of God, and the angel of death would pass them by. Death took the firstborn of every Egyptian family at midnight. But the angel of death passed over the homes of the Israelite families. The feast of the Passover is still an important Jewish holy day.

When at last Pharaoh understood the true power of God, he agreed to let the people go. But even then, Pharaoh had a change of heart and sent his army after the Israelites. Moses helped the Israelites escape by parting the Red Sea, through the power of God, allowing the Israelites to cross and preventing Pharaoh's guards from following them. After centuries of slavery, the Israelites were free.

Though God would always grant their requests, the Israelites quickly forgot how much God had done for them, and they started worshiping idols. They would only turn back to God when threatened with death. The forty years they wandered in the wilderness is a story of human promises made and broken—and a story of God's faithfulness in the face of people's unfaithfulness. When they reached the Promised Land at last, the relationship between God and the Israelites had become a vital part of their worship and their history.

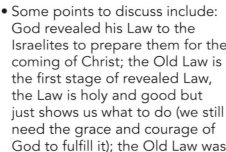

- *Do you find yourself turning to God only when you need something?*
- *Why is it so easy to overlook the things God does for us?*

God's People as Community

"I will raise up your offspring after you...and I will establish his kingdom. He it is who shall build a house for my name, and I will establish his royal throne forever. I will be a father to him, and he shall be a son to me."

2 Samuel 7:12–14

After Moses, God's people began to see their journey as that of a community. God was the head of this community, but when the people continued to be unfaithful, God sent female and male judges to guide them. Through bravery and wisdom, these judges sometimes saved Israel from being conquered.

The people begged God to send them a king, even though God warned them that a king would not be as generous as God. The first king, Saul, grew jealous of the popularity of a young shepherd boy, David, and tried to have him murdered (1 Samuel 19). While David was forced to flee for his life several times, he continued to show mercy to Saul and Saul's descendants.

When David was finally proclaimed king after Saul's death (2 Samuel 2), he led his people to years of prosperity, yet his own life was filled with tragedy. His sons betrayed him, and he selfishly committed the sin of adultery and murder. Unlike Saul, David admitted his sinfulness and asked God for forgiveness. God promised his kingdom would never end and that one of David's descendants "will be a son to me." This promise to David hints at the new covenant that would be fulfilled in Jesus, the Son of God.

Israel in Captivity

David's son, Solomon, turned Israel into a powerful nation and built the first Temple in Jerusalem. But Solomon became too attached to worldly things and began worshiping other gods. He lost touch with the one, true God. As a result of Solomon's unfaithfulness, the kingdom was split in two. Israel became the kingdom in the north and Judah in the south. These two kingdoms often warred against each other, and the people continued to worship false gods.

C10

God's People as Community

- Read the verse from 2 Samuel aloud. Ask participants what it makes them think of or what it might be referring to.

Suggested responses: It could be referring to the promise of Jesus and the New Covenant, Jesus will establish the eternal kingdom by becoming fully human....

- Emphasize how the old covenant and Old Testament build up to the new covenant in Jesus. You may find it helpful to go over paragraphs 1961–64 in the *Catechism* with participants.

- Some points to discuss include: God revealed his Law to the Israelites to prepare them for the coming of Christ; the Old Law is the first stage of revealed Law, the Law is holy and good but just shows us what to do (we still need the grace and courage of God to fulfill it); the Old Law was preparation for the Gospel.

Israel in Captivity

- Ask participants why they think it's important for Christians to understand the history of their faith and the faith of their Jewish ancestors.

Suggested response: The Gospel and New Covenant was built on the old, we have to understand where God's people started before we can fully understand the New Testament.

- Emphasize important themes in Hebrew Scripture such as God's faithfulness and God's mercy and forgiveness; themes still paramount to Church teachings today.

For each of the following biblical figures list what they are best known for and something you can learn from their example. Look up their stories in the Old Testament for help. Abraham, Joseph, Moses, David, John the Baptist (the New Testament).

Suggested responses include:

- Abraham
  Becomes the father of nations. Shows great faithfulness and trust in God.

- Joseph
  Saves Egypt and his family from great famine. Shows great forgiveness and mercy toward the brothers who betrayed him.

- Moses
  Leads the Israelites out of slavery in Egypt. Shows great leadership through his trust in God.

- David
  Leads the Israelites in prosperity. Shows great humility by admitting his sins and asking God for forgiveness.

- John the Baptist
  Proclaims Jesus' coming and baptizes Jesus in the Jordan River. Shows great faith in Jesus and acknowledges Jesus as God.

Many prophets warned the people to reform and return to living the covenant made with God. The warnings of the prophets fell on deaf ears. The kings listened instead to false prophets who told them all was well (2 Chronicles 18:5–34).

In 587 BC, the Babylonians captured Jerusalem, the capital of Judah. A few people remained faithful to God and began to hope for the time when they would be reconciled to God. In exile in Babylon, the Israelites finally began to form the image of themselves as a people held together by God. Several legends of heroism came out of this period, many of them about great women like Esther (Book of Esther) and Susanna (Book of Daniel).

When Cyrus conquered Babylon, God inspired him to let the Israelites return to their land and rebuild their Temple. This period of rebuilding lasted about 200 years. Then the Israelites were conquered by Alexander the Great, and they again came under foreign rule. From 63 BC, the Roman Empire controlled the region and allowed the Temple in Jerusalem to be rebuilt, though on a smaller scale. The Israelites' desire for reconciliation with God once again grew with the appearance of the desert prophet, John the Baptist, who proclaimed the coming of the Messiah, "the one who is coming after me is mightier than I" (Matthew 3:11).

As the new covenant, Jesus fulfills God's promise to Adam and Eve and to Abraham and Sarah. Jesus restores David's kingdom, though in new glory, much different from that anticipated by the Israelites.

For each of the following biblical figures, list what they are best known for and something you can learn from their example.

Look up their stories in the Old Testament for help:

Abraham	Joseph
Moses	David
Cyrus	John the Baptist (New Testament)

Compare your personal faith journey with the faith journey of the Israelites.

When in your life have you been closest to God? Where are you now?

Journey of Faith for Teens: Catechumenate, C10 (826290)
Imprimi Potest: Stephen T. Rehrauer, CSsR, Provincial, Denver Province, the Redemptorists.
Imprimatur: "In accordance with CIC 827, permission to publish has been granted on March 23, 2016, by the Most Reverend Edward M. Rice, Auxiliary Bishop, Archdiocese of St. Louis. Permission to publish is an indication that nothing contrary to Church teaching is contained in this work. It does not imply any endorsement of the opinions expressed in the publication, nor is any liability assumed by this permission."
Journey of Faith © 2000, 2016 Liguori Publications, Liguori, MO 63057. To order, visit Liguori.org or call 800-325-9521. Liguori Publications, a nonprofit corporation, is an apostolate of the Redemptorists. To learn more about the Redemptorists, visit Redemptorists.com. All rights reserved. No part of this publication may be reproduced, distributed, stored, transmitted, or posted in any form by any means without prior written permission. Text: Adapted from *Journey of Faith* © 2000 Liguori Publications. Editors of 2016 *Journey of Faith:* Theresa Nienaber and Pat Fosarelli, MD, DMin. Design: Lorena Mitre Jimenez. Images: Shutterstock.
Unless noted, Scripture texts in this work are taken from *New American Bible*, revised edition © 2010, 1991, 1986, 1970 Confraternity of Christian Doctrine, Washington, D.C., and are used by permission of the copyright owner. All Rights Reserved. No part of *New American Bible* may be reproduced in any form without permission in writing from the copyright owner. Excerpts from English translation of the *Catechism of the Catholic Church* for the United States of America © 1994 United States Catholic Conference, Inc. —Libreria Editrice Vaticana; English translation of the *Catechism of the Catholic Church: Modifications from the Editio Typica* © 1997 United States Catholic Conference, Inc. —Libreria Editrice Vaticana. Compliant with *The Roman Missal, Third Edition.*
Printed in the United States of America. 20 19 18 17 16 / 5 4 3 2 1. Third Edition.

LIGUORI
PUBLICATIONS
A Redemptorist Ministry

Journaling

Compare your personal faith journey with the faith journey of the Israelites. When in your life have you been closest to God? Where are you now?

Closing Prayer

After the participants have expressed any personal intentions, pray the Our Father and Glory Be together as a closing prayer.

Looking Ahead

The Old Testament lays a foundation for the new covenant we receive in Jesus Christ. Before the next lesson, ask participants to think about what it means for God to have entered into a new covenant for us and what that might have meant for the early church.

Catechism: 425, 748–776, 858

Objectives

- Outline the development of the Christian Church from Pentecost through Emperor Constantine.

- Compare and contrast the ministries of Sts. Peter and Paul.

- Identify persecution as a common trial for the early Church.

Leader Meditation

Matthew 10:5–42

Read and reflect on the mission of the Twelve Apostles. How is the mission of the Twelve similar to your own mission as Christ's witness? When have you felt like a sheep among wolves? When have you felt comforted by Christ's words "Even the hairs of your head are all counted. So do not be afraid?"

Leader Preparation

- Read the lesson, this lesson plan, the Scripture passage, and the *Catechism* sections.

- You may want to bring in extra copies of the *Catechism of the Catholic Church* and Bibles for the activity.

- Be familiar with the vocabulary terms for this lesson: commission, Pentecost, presbyters. Definitions are provided in this guide's glossary.

Welcome

Greet participants as they arrive. Check for supplies and immediate needs. Solicit questions or comments about the previous session and/or share new information and findings. Begin promptly.

Opening Scripture

Matthew 10:5–25

Ask for a volunteer to light the candle and read aloud. Point out especially Jesus' instructions to proclaim the good news, cure the sick, and give without payment. Before beginning your discussion of the lesson handout, discuss with participants **how they've seen Catholics today going out and being disciples of Jesus.**

> The apostles' ministry is the continuation of [Jesus'] mission; Jesus said to the Twelve: "he who receives you receives me." *CCC 858*

Journey of Faith

The Early Church

Following his high-school graduation, Max wasn't sure what he wanted to do with his life. All his friends saw college as a great new beginning, but Max couldn't decide if college was the right choice for him. He couldn't imagine himself enjoying any of the careers chosen by his friends.

Max's one true love was music. He played the guitar well. Every minute he could spare, Max played his guitar, wishing he could somehow build his future around it. Max decided to postpone college for a year. He found a job as a teacher's aide working with young children who had learning and behavioral difficulties. Instinctively, Max took his guitar to work with him, thinking the kids might enjoy hearing him play.

Almost immediately, the children grew very fond of Max and his music. The teacher began using Max and his guitar as a reward for good behavior, and soon the children were working well above her expectations. At Christmas, the class entertained the school with a holiday music program.

Max went on to pursue a degree in special education with a minor in music. Today he is known for setting up resource programs for children with learning disabilities in Catholic grade schools. Max never could have imagined where his new beginning would lead him, but his guitar still goes with him—everywhere.

- *How did Max decide what he wanted to do with his future?*
- *How have you been changed by new experiences?*

When faced with his new beginning, Max was confused and unsure of the future. We've all experienced times when the future seems frightening or uncertain.

Whatever your new beginning, you probably had no idea where you would end up. But you had to take that first step. Two thousand years ago, the Church was in the same position. Not one of those early Church members could begin to imagine the Church of today when they first started out. If the early Church had stayed the way it was back then, we would still be a small part of the Jewish faith.

But like Max, the Church moved forward, one step at a time. Like Max, early Church leaders felt uncertain about their future. It took courage to face that new beginning.

It's clear from the New Testament that Jesus founded the Church to be a community for his followers. He chose a group to follow after him, his apostles. Simon was renamed Peter (which means rock) because he was to be the foundation of Christ's Church. The apostles were given a **commission** (a special purpose or mission) to carry the good news of Jesus' life, death, and

CCC 425, 748–776, 858

The Early Church

- After reading the story of Max, ask participants how they have been changed by new experiences. Discuss the courage it takes to grow through a new beginning.

- Emphasize that the early Church parallels our personal faith (and growing-up) journey: uncertainty, trials, change, and tremendous growth.

- Explain the meaning and importance of the word *commissioned*—to be given a special purpose or mission—and that as baptized Christians we are commissioned by Jesus as well.

- Discuss how participants start a task or mission they feel unprepared for.

- Ask how they think the early apostles might have begun their mission. Emphasize that the early apostles probably made some mistakes, too.

The Start of the Church

- Have participants read Acts 2:1–33. If you're short on time, divide participants into three groups and have each group answer one of the three questions:

  o When have you felt scared like the apostles in the upper room?

  o When have you felt like the apostles, inspired by the Spirit?

  o Find a verse from Peter's speech that stands out to you; which did you choose and why?

While there are no right or wrong answers to these questions, encourage participants to be honest about themselves and their faith journey. Encourage them to take comfort knowing even those closest to Jesus were sometimes scared and uncertain in their faith, but that Jesus always provided them with the courage and grace they needed to keep going.

---

resurrection to the farthest ends of the earth. Our Lord promised to remain with this community of believers until the end of time.

"In Christian usage, the word 'church' designates the liturgical assembly, but also the local community or the whole universal community of believers....'The Church' is the People that God gathers in the whole world. She exists in local communities and is made real as a liturgical, above all a Eucharistic, assembly."

CCC 752

The first Christians didn't inherit an organization with ready-made laws and a book of instructions on how it should operate. All they had to go on was Jesus' example when he led and preached on earth. Only through time, by responding to the problems and needs of everyday life and by being open to the guidance of the Holy Spirit would the early Christian leaders come to understand the direction in which God was leading them.

- Have you ever had to do something you felt totally unprepared for? How'd you do it?

The Start of the Church

"And they were all filled with the holy Spirit and began to speak in different tongues, as the Spirit enabled them to proclaim."

Acts 2:4

The descent of the Holy Spirit upon Jesus' disciples on **Pentecost** is celebrated as the birthday of the Church. After Jesus ascended into heaven, the disciples went to the upper room and prayed. They were full of fear and felt very uncertain about their future. They wondered what was expected of them and how they could possibly carry out the great commission Jesus had given them.

In spite of doubts and fears, the mighty power of God became very real when all of them were filled with the courage and strength of the Holy Spirit. We don't know exactly how the Spirit influenced these disciples, but we do know that their hearts underwent an incredible and unexplainable transformation. By the power of the Spirit, these frightened people, huddled in the safety of the upper room, were suddenly transformed into courageous beings unafraid to proclaim the Good News to everyone they met. Scripture tells us that a large number of Jews came to Christ that day.

Read Acts 2:1–33, the story of Pentecost.

- When have you felt scared like the apostles were in the upper room?

- When have you felt like the apostles, inspired by the spirit?

- Read Peter's speech closely. Find a verse that stands out to you. Which did you choose and why?

Christians or Jews?

Sometimes we talk about discovering who we really are, about finding ourselves, about seeking our true identity.

Christians went through a similar experience during the early years of the Church. The converts to Christ did not feel cut off from other Jews. They simply felt that they lived in the fulfillment of the Old Testament. The long-awaited Messiah had finally come. These early Christians faithfully went to the Temple to worship God, their "Lord and Christ."

Nevertheless, they were different. The fact that they saw Jesus Christ as the Messiah eventually became a clear division between the Jewish and Christian faiths. Though Christ's followers frequented the Temple, they also met privately in their homes for "the breaking of bread," the sacrifice Jesus had left them. This Eucharist was the bond that would hold them together. In sharing in his Body, they themselves became the body that is the Church.

- Has your desire to be a Catholic ever made you feel isolated or separated? Part of a community?

Christians or Jews?

- If time allows, answer the reflection question as a group. If participants hesitate to share their own experiences, try sharing one of your own to stimulate conversation or rephrase the question and ask, "Why might Catholics sometimes feel separated or isolated because of their faith? How does sharing a universal faith make us part of a community?"

Suggested responses include: Not everyone we meet will understand or respect our faith. Sometimes our faith requires us to act in unpopular ways or hold unpopular opinions. Being Catholic unites us as the Body of Christ. Sharing a faith allows us to connect in a special way to Catholics all of the world....

When Did the Separation from Judaism Occur?

"The Church, and through her the world, will not be perfected in glory without great trials."

CCC 769

Judaism and Christianity lived side by side for a while, but eventually the two faiths became divided over small questions of how to live their faith. Some of these disagreements included whether or not Gentiles needed to convert to Judaism before becoming Christian or whether or not Gentile Christian men needed to be circumcised.

Persecution broke out against the community of Christ in Jerusalem (see Acts 8:1). But God brought good out of the persecution; it forced many Christians to leave Jerusalem and go into the world, taking the good news of Jesus with them.

The Holy Spirit also showed the Christian community that the salvation of Christ was for all people, not just for Jews. This set the stage for another new beginning. A zealous Pharisee named Saul, who was determined to crush the young Christian communities, was miraculously converted by God (see Acts 9:1–9). Saul became the great St. Paul.

Paul was the one God called to preach to the Gentiles, people who were non-Jews. In Paul's missions, he preached the good news of Christ first to the Jews, but if they rejected him, he went to the Gentiles. Many Jews saw him as a traitor and rejected him, but he also gained many converts to the Christian faith.

Different Views of Christianity

"For though languages differ throughout the world, the content of the Tradition is one and the same. The Churches established in Germany have no other faith or Tradition, nor do those of the Iberians, nor those of the Celts, nor those of the East, of Egypt, of Libya."

CCC 174

As Christianity grew, it started to reach many cultures that looked at this new religion from different points of view. Salvation was not and is not limited to one way of understanding reality. Jesus came for all people. He came so that all the ends of the earth might see the power and love of God.

For Greeks, interested in philosophy, Christianity had to be understood in terms of metaphysics, which attempts to understand and describe the origin and structure of the universe. Jesus was the wisdom of God made flesh and the communicator of divine wisdom. This community placed great emphasis on creeds and dogma (principles of belief).

Rome, with its great tradition of justice and law, gave Christianity an inheritance of morals. Christ was the greatest of all lawgivers. As a result, ethics and morals became central to the faith. Jesus was the perfect man.

The rapid spread of Christianity was due primarily to a God who gives faith, strength, and vision to believers. People were hungry for a faith that gave meaning to their lives and offered hope in the face of death. Because the Roman Empire's gods did not foster any sense of morality or neighborly love, many people gladly opened their hearts to receive the good news of Christ when they heard it.

Why Were Christians Persecuted?

When Rome burned in the year 64, Emperor Nero had to save himself from the anger of the people, so he blamed the Christians for the destruction. Nero had Christians crucified and ignited as human torches. He decreed that no one could profess a belief in Christianity. It was during Nero's persecution that both Peter and Paul died for Christ. Though it seems that Christian martyrs may have numbered in the millions, they were not continually under persecution for the next few centuries.

The early Church also had to deal with disagreement from inside. Many Christians denied their faith to save their lives. Then when persecution subsided, they would want to return to the Church. The decision over how to handle this divided many Christian communities, although the approved approach was to accept them back as people who must do penance.

Why Were Christians Persecuted?

- As you discuss the persecution of early Christians, ask participants if they've ever felt separated or isolated because of their faith. Have they ever been afraid of how friends would react if they admitted to being practicing Christians?

- Then discuss how early Christians formed communities. Ask participants how they experience community with the Church. Emphasize those shared rituals we still have in common with the early Christians (*the Eucharist, listening to God's word, baptism...*).

With a partner or as a group, put yourself in the position of those early Christians. Discuss how you might have handled the common struggles of the early Church (such as persecution, Christians who denied their faith out of fear, or establishing Church leadership). Are there issues you see the Church struggling with today? How can today's Church work to overcome them? If you need help getting started, use a Bible or the *Catechism*.

Despite persecution from without and disagreement from within, the life of the Church developed. Converts, after lengthy instruction, were baptized, usually by immersion in a river. The ritual of the breaking of bread, the Mass, bound the Christian community together in the real Body and Blood of Jesus.

If a Christian community grew large enough, the bishop would ordain **presbyters** (priests) to assist him. Deacons, besides instructing, saw to the various charities of the Church and distributed the Eucharist. The bishops who succeeded Peter as bishop of Rome (the pope) continued to have authority in the Church. Though the government of the Church was not centralized as it is today, there is much evidence that the bishop of Rome was looked to for authority.

The persecution of Christians continued until Constantine, the western emperor, defeated his rival, Maxentius, and in 313 decreed tolerance toward Christianity. At long last, Christians could practice their faith without fear of persecution.

But this freedom, too, was only another new beginning.

With a partner or as a group, put yourself in the position of those early Christians. Discuss how you might have handled the common struggles of the early Church, such as persecution, Christians who denied their faith out of fear, or establishing Church leadership.

Are there issues you see the Church struggling with today? How can today's Church work to overcome them? If you need help getting started, use a Bible or the *Catechism*.

Think of an example from your own life when you had to make a new beginning.

What happened?

Journey of Faith for Teens: Catechumenate, C11 (826290)
Imprimi Potest: Stephen T. Rehrauer, CSsR, Provincial, Denver Province, the Redemptorists.
Imprimatur: "In accordance with CIC 827, permission to publish has been granted on March 23, 2016, by the Most Reverend Edward M. Rice, Auxiliary Bishop, Archdiocese of St. Louis. Permission to publish is an indication that nothing contrary to Church teaching is contained in this work. It does not imply any endorsement of the opinions expressed in the publication; nor is any liability assumed by this permission."
Journey of Faith © 2000, 2016 Liguori Publications, Liguori, MO 63057. To order, visit Liguori.org or call 800-325-9521. Liguori Publications, a nonprofit corporation, is an apostolate of the Redemptorists. To learn more about the Redemptorists, visit Redemptorists.com. All rights reserved. No part of this publication may be reproduced, distributed, stored, transmitted, or posted in any form by any means without prior written permission. Text: Adapted from *Journey of Faith* © 2000 Liguori Publications. Editors of 2016 *Journey of Faith*: Theresa Nienaber and Pat Fosarelli, MD, DMin. Design: Lorena Mitre Jimenez. Images: Shutterstock. Unless noted, Scripture texts in this work are taken from *New American Bible*, revised edition. © 2010, 1991, 1986, 1970 Confraternity of Christian Doctrine, Washington, D.C. and are used by permission of the copyright owner. All Rights Reserved. No part of *New American Bible* may be reproduced in any form without permission in writing from the copyright owner. Excerpts from English translation of the *Catechism of the Catholic Church* for the United States of America © 1994 United States Catholic Conference, Inc.—*Libreria Editrice Vaticana*. English translation of the *Catechism of the Catholic Church: Modifications from the Editio Typica* © 1997 United States Catholic Conference, Inc.—*Libreria Editrice Vaticana*. Compliant with *The Roman Missal, Third Edition*.
Printed in the United States of America. 20 19 18 17 16 / 5 4 3 2 1. Third Edition.

Liguori PUBLICATIONS
A Redemptorist Ministry

Journaling

Think of an example from your own life when you had to make a new beginning. What happened?

Closing Prayer

After acknowledging any special intentions, read the Apostles' Creed as a closing prayer. If you have only one copy of the Creed, you may wish to pass it around the group, allowing each participant to read a few lines and then pass it on.

Take-home

Ask participants to reflect on what actions or rituals were part of the lives of early Christians the next time they go to Mass. Have participants reflect on this connection and what it means to them.

C12: Church History

Catechism: 811–870

Objectives

- Describe major historical milestones in Church history, such as the Crusades, the Reformation, and Vatican II.
- List major saints and religious orders who helped shape today's Church.
- Recognize the Spirit remains with, guides, and protects the Church.

Leader Meditation

Matthew 28:16–20

With these words from Matthew, Jesus breathed life into his Church. The same words still hold us together today, giving life to the Church. Hear Jesus saying these words to you. Share this amazing truth with each participant in your RCIA class today. The Lord who leads the Church promises to be with each one of us every day.

Leader Preparation

- Read the lesson, this lesson plan, the Scripture passage, and the *Catechism* sections.
- Be familiar with the vocabulary terms for this lesson: heresy, martyrdom, missionary, denomination. Definitions are provided in this guide's glossary.

Welcome

Greet participants as they arrive. Check for supplies and immediate needs. Solicit questions or comments about the previous session and/or share new information and findings. Begin promptly.

Opening Scripture

Matthew 28:16–20

Ask a volunteer to light the candle and read aloud. Before beginning your discussion of the lesson handout, discuss these questions with participants: **Do you think this message was only for the apostles? Or was it also directed to all of us?**

> The Church, endowed with the gifts of her founder and faithfully observing his precepts of charity, humility and self-denial, receives the mission of proclaiming and establishing among all peoples the Kingdom of Christ and of God, and she is on earth the seed and the beginning of that kingdom.
>
> *CCC 768*

In Short:

- The Church has a varied and rich history.
- Saints and religious orders helped shape the Church.
- The Holy Spirit guides the Church.

Church History

Kathleen found a puppy near the side of the road. He lay huddled next to his lifeless companion, likely a sibling. Kathleen could only guess that the puppies had been abandoned. The faithful brother would not leave his sibling's side, despite the fact he was terrified.

It took months for Kathleen to earn the puppy's trust after she brought him home that night. She named the pup Second Chance because she was hoping she could give him exactly that—a second chance. She called him Chance.

Kathleen wished she knew her dog's history, thinking that might help her understand him better. Without knowing the exact details of Chance's history, Kathleen could only assume his puppyhood had been one of neglect and abuse. She knew it would take years for Chance to fully trust her. But she vowed to give her dog a second chance at a happy, love-filled life.

- How does knowing something's history help you understand it better?

Why Is History Important?

Your life story reflects who you are and what's happened to make you who you are. Anyone who wants to get to know you needs to learn about your history, too. It's the same with the Catholic Church. The story of the Church, like your own personal story, is the story of a journey of faith. The Church's journey began thousands of years ago with the Israelites, had its foundation in Jesus Christ, and has evolved through many periods, some of them extremely difficult.

What Happened After Christianity Became Acceptable?

When we left the early Church in lesson C11 ("Early Church"), it was just getting through a period of great persecution. Now freed from that fear and anxiety, Christians had time to think about the truths of God's revelation made through Jesus Christ. Many great thinkers expanded the Church's understanding of God. Unfortunately, this period in Church history also produced some thinkers whose thoughts wandered far from the course set by Jesus during his earthly ministry.

Heresies, beliefs or opinions that directly contradict official Church teaching, emerged. One heresy said Jesus was not divine; another said Jesus was not human. Some emperors supported heresies, and some Christians were executed for disagreeing with them.

Even with these challenges, **martyrdom** (the giving of one's life for the sake of one's faith) declined as Christianity became more acceptable in the empire. Christians were able to find new ways to dedicate their lives to Jesus. Many chose

CCC 811–870

What Happened After Christianity Became Acceptable?

- If time allows, discuss the reflection questions as a group.

- How would being part of a community help strengthen the desire to live like Christ?

Suggested responses include: You'd have the influence and support of other Christians, you'd be able to continuously learn about your faith, you'd have others to look to for inspiration, and more…

- Would it be hard (or easy) to live the Christian life in isolation?

Suggested responses include: It might be easier because you'd have less temptation from outside sources, it might be more difficult because you'd have to live alone without the support of others, and so on…

Church History

- Read the introduction and ask the participants how knowing someone's (or something's) history helps you understand them (or it) better.

Suggested responses include: You start to understand why they react differently to experiences or events; you may learn why they do things a certain way; you can have a better appreciation for how something has become what it is because you know what it took to get there, and so on….

Why Is History Important?

- Ask participants to reflect on their own histories of faith. You can use these questions to prompt their reflection: *Were they always Christians? Did they doubt God? What influenced them to look at the Catholic Church?* Allow participants to share if they're willing, or share your own faith history and what led you to teach RCIA classes.

- Emphasize that while the Church has a long history, the Church is not stagnant but continues to grow.

Changes in the Roman Empire

- Discuss how Church history has influenced the Church. Emphasize how Church leaders are human. This means some have done great things to help build up the Church but others have made wrong or selfish choices.

- Discuss how the Church can still be of God even though Christians sin.

Suggested responses include: While the Christians are human and prone to sin, the teachings and truth of the Church come from God. These teachings are infallible and God, through his Spirit, ensures that even when Christians or Church leaders fall into sin, these truths remain pure.

- If this question raises concern or confusion among participants, refer to *Catechism* paragraphs 2032–2040. If you have time, you can read this section as a class or suggest participants read it on their own.

to go to the desert. These men and women felt that the solitary life kept them away from society's corruption. Religious communities were formed as people began to gather around these holy men and women, creating intentional communities focused on living a life of prayer and service. Other Christians turned to social services, providing care and compassion to the poor, sick, dying, and abandoned.

- *How would being part of a community help strengthen the desire to live like Christ?*

- *Would it be hard or easy to live the Christian life in isolation?*

Changes in the Roman Empire

In the fifth century, the Roman Empire began to collapse as barbarian tribes invaded. Bishops became the only authorities people could rely on. At first, Roman Christians wanted nothing to do with the barbarian conquerors, but eventually they began to feel the call to convert the invaders.

These were the first **missionaries**. Missionary men and women work to bring the faith to unbelievers, often through social service. To bring the newly converted to a deeper knowledge of Christianity, monasteries and parishes were founded. The highly educated monks helped instruct the people, while parishes made Christianity the center of community life. Clergy (ordained Church officials) were employed by the invaders as ambassadors and public leaders. Service to the poor was almost completely up to the Church.

However, there were also serious problems that arose because of the close ties between Church and state. Nobles appointed bishops, often choosing someone who would support their interests rather than the gospel. Priests were appointed by local landowners and had little or no training. Many became more interested in material possessions and power than in spreading the good news.

- *How has history influenced the way the Church functions?*

- *Can the Church still do good even if Christians sin?*

Back to Basics

The eleventh and twelfth centuries saw the flowering of great universities, Gothic architecture, and extraordinary thinkers and scholars. These centuries also brought new problems to the Church. In 1054, disagreement about the pope's role and a difference in understanding of how we talk about the Holy Spirit in the Creed led to a *schism* or division of the Eastern (Orthodox) Church from Rome.

Saint Bernard (1090–1153) and others brought reform to religious communities, asking them to return to a life of prayer. Their reform spread throughout the rest of the Church. Finally, Pope Gregory VII took back the power to appoint clergy from the nobles.

In addition to the noble desire to protect Christianity's holy sites, the less noble feeling of greed and a desire for power fueled the Crusades (1095–1291). In a series of military expeditions, Christians of western Europe attempted to take Jerusalem and the Holy Land from the Muslims.

While the Crusades continued through most of the thirteenth century, the Church of this time also had people of remarkable character. Saints Francis of Assisi and Dominic changed the way Christianity was preached. Monasteries preserved the teachings of the Church but had lost contact with the common people who needed this knowledge. Francis, Dominic, and their followers took the gospel message to the streets and lived simply among the people.

The Call for Reform

The fourteenth and fifteenth centuries were fraught with confusion. At times, two and three men claimed to be pope. Corruption among many Church leaders and interference in the Church by secular authorities increased. Saint Catherine of Siena and others called for renewal.

In 1517, Martin Luther, a Catholic monk, called for an end to the abuses in the Church. He wanted reform, as many other Catholics did, not a new Church. Yet poor communication, stubbornness on both sides, and interference by secular authorities led him to take a "protestant" position and break away from Catholicism. Division followed division, and Christianity has since split into thousands of denominations.

This *Protestant Reformation* shocked the Catholic leadership into action. The Council of Trent (1545–1563) clarified Catholic belief, corrected abuses, and set up the seminary system to educate clergy. New religious orders began to help in renewal and promotion of spiritual growth.

• *How does an emphasis on social service show the Church's roots in Jesus' ministry?*

The Call to Service

Social service and everyday spirituality were the focus of the seventeenth and eighteenth centuries. Saint Francis de Sales wrote books that called laypeople to holiness. Saints Vincent de Paul and Louise de Marillac organized ways to help the poor. They set up groups of laypeople, called "confraternities," to manage orphanages, homes for the elderly, and parish services for the needy.

Catholicism in America

In the United States, Catholics were a small and insignificant number in the early 1800s. By the 1860s, they comprised the largest single religious group, or **denomination**, in the United States, numbering three and a half million people.

This increase in numbers was the result of large numbers of immigrants coming from Ireland and Germany. Later, many Catholics from Poland, Italy, and Hispanic countries also came to America.

The birth of modern Catholic social teaching came as the result of the Industrial Revolution. In 1891, Pope Leo XIII spoke out in support of the rights of working people. He believed in a worker's right to a fair wage, the right to form associations (unions), and the right to go on strike to defend workers' rights.

A **denomination** in Christianity is a distinct religious body with its own ways of worship, leadership, and doctrine. Historically, many of these denominations broke away from the Catholic Church.

The Church in the Twentieth Century

"The joys and the hopes, the griefs and the anxieties of the men of this age, especially those who are poor or in any way afflicted, these are the joys and hopes, the griefs and anxieties of the followers of Christ."

Pastoral Constitution on the Church in the Modern World *(Gaudium et Spes)*, 1

In the 1960s, the Second Vatican Council—an important gathering in Rome of Catholic bishops worldwide, as well as laypeople and leaders from other Christian communities—took a close look at the modern Church. The council made many changes in the ways Catholics worship and practice their faith. It encouraged laypeople to become more involved in the work of the Church and to renew their efforts to follow Christ.

Ministries that were once the work of only priests are now carried out by laypeople in part because of renewed efforts to engage the laity in the Mass, but also because of a decrease in the number of priests. At Mass, laypeople proclaim the word (the priest or deacon still proclaims the Gospel), distribute holy Communion, lead the assembly in song, and serve as ministers of hospitality. Most parishes have active liturgical committees that involve laypeople in planning liturgical feasts and celebrations.

The Church Today

Today's Church takes a strong stand on moral and social issues, such as abortion and assisted suicide, which ignore Christ's teachings regarding the sacredness and priceless value of human life. The Church remains very active in aiding the poor of the world and in offering support to those who suffer from other forms of poverty. You'll discuss this part of the Church's mission more in lesson C16, "Social Justice."

There are many challenges facing the Church today, as there have been throughout its history. As we face these challenges and try to learn from past mistakes, it is important to remember that we are all human, as imperfect as the apostles before us. Yet the Church is still the body of Christ, and we can trust that the Holy Spirit will continue to guide us.

The Call to Service

• Ask participants why an emphasis on service and community is important to build and maintain the Church Jesus founded.

  o *"Because they are members of the Body whose Head is Christ, Christians contribute to building up the Church by the constancy of their convictions and their moral lives. The Church increases, grows, and develops through the holiness of her faithful"* (CCC 2045).

The Church in the Twentieth Century

• Discuss the important changes in Church thinking that resulted from the Second Vatican Council.

Suggested responses include: the role of the layperson; emphasis on making liturgy meaningful to people in their own language and culture; the importance of social service.

The Church Today

• Talk about the challenges facing the Catholic Church and many other Christian churches today.

Suggested responses include: materialism, a rise in secularism, the widespread practice and acceptance of abortion, and so on...).

• Ask participants how they live Christian values in their own lives or what advice they'd give to other young Christians in the face of these modern challenges.

As a group, make a list of the ways the Church today reaches people with the good news and the effects of that outreach. Make another list of ways you wish the Church were more active and what results those ways might have.

As a group, list the ways the Church today reaches people with the good news and the effects of that outreach. Make another list of ways you wish the Church were more active and what effects those ways might have.

Recall a time when you made a mistake.

What did this mistake teach you about yourself? How did it help you grow? Become more understanding or forgiving? How did it influence who you are today?

Journey of Faith for Teens: Catechumenate, C12 (826290)
Imprimi Potest: Stephen T. Rehrauer, CSsR, Provincial, Denver Province, the Redemptorists.
Imprimatur: "In accordance with CIC 827, permission to publish has been granted on March 23, 2016, by the Most Reverend Edward M. Rice, Auxiliary Bishop, Archdiocese of St. Louis. Permission to publish is an indication that nothing contrary to Church teaching is contained in this work. It does not imply any endorsement of the opinions expressed in the publication, nor is any liability assumed by this permission."
Journey of Faith © 2000, 2016 Liguori Publications, Liguori, MO 63057. To order, visit Liguori.org or call 800-325-9521. Liguori Publications, a nonprofit corporation, is an apostolate of the Redemptorists. To learn more about the Redemptorists, visit Redemptorists.com. All rights reserved. No part of this publication may be reproduced, distributed, stored, transmitted, or posted in any form by any means without prior written permission. Text: Adapted from *Journey of Faith* © 2000 Liguori Publications.
Editors of 2016 *Journey of Faith:* Theresa Nienaber and Pat Fosarelli, MD, DMin. Design: Lorena Mitre Jimenez. Images: Shutterstock. Unless noted, Scripture texts in this work are taken from *New American Bible,* revised edition. © 2010, 1991, 1986, 1970 Confraternity of Christian Doctrine, Washington, D.C., and are used by permission of the copyright owner. All Rights Reserved. No part of *New American Bible* may be reproduced in any form without permission in writing from the copyright owner. Excerpts from English translation of the *Catechism of the Catholic Church* for the United States of America © 1994 United States Catholic Conference, Inc. —Libreria Editrice Vaticana; English translation of the *Catechism of the Catholic Church: Modifications from the Editio Typica* © 1997 United States Catholic Conference, Inc. —Libreria Editrice Vaticana. Compliant with *The Roman Missal, Third Edition.* Printed in the United States of America. 20 19 18 17 16 / 5 4 3 2 1. Third Edition.

Liguori PUBLICATIONS
A Redemptorist Ministry

Journaling

Recall a time when you made a mistake. What did this mistake teach you about yourself? How did it help you grow? Did it help you become more understanding or forgiving? How did it influence who you are today?

Closing Prayer

After asking for special intentions, pray the Lord's Prayer together. Keep in mind that this prayer has been with the Church throughout its history.

Looking Ahead

As participants prepare for the next class, ask them to think more about the Church today. What is it known for? How does it interact with the community? How does the Church encourage them to act in the world as Christians?

C13: Christian Moral Living

Catechism: 1776–1832

Objectives

- Discover morality is based on natural law but ordered by Christ.
- Recognize disciples are called to form their consciences according to Church teaching.
- Reflect on personal choices and behaviors with an eye toward conversion and expressing greater love for God and others.

Leader Meditation

Proverbs 3:5–6

It can be easy for us to look at other people and think, *"Well, at least I'm not doing that."* But when we "trust in the LORD" we have to do more than rely on our own interpretations of right and wrong. We have to interpret the world the way Jesus sees us. It's often the most difficult situations and the hardest choices that require us to rely on ourselves the least and God the most. When have you needed the Church to help you make difficult choices? Has it been hard to follow the Church's teaching in these moments?

Leader Preparation

- Read the lesson, this lesson plan, the Scripture passage, and the *Catechism* sections.
- You may also want to have the Ten Commandments visible somewhere in the room for this lesson or have your Bible open to Exodus 20:1–17.
- Consider using the song "Restless" (Audrey Assad and Matt Maher, from *The House You're Building*, Sparrow) for your closing prayer.
- Be familiar with the vocabulary terms for this lesson: commandments, conscience, free will. Definitions are provided in this guide's glossary.

Welcome

Greet participants as they arrive. Check for supplies and immediate needs. Solicit questions or comments about the previous session and/or share new information and findings. Begin promptly.

Opening Scripture

Matthew 22:34–40

Ask a volunteer to light the candle and read aloud. Allow a few moments for silent reflection. Before beginning your discussion of the lesson handout, discuss with participants **why might it be easier to just obey the rules than live and act with love.**

> The Ten Commandments are engraved by God in the human heart. *CCC 2072*

In Short:

- Morality is ultimately ordered by Christ.
- We are called to reflect on personal choices.
- We are called to form our conscience.

"Deep within his conscience man discovers a law which he has not laid upon himself but which he must obey. Its voice, ever calling him to love and to do what is good and to avoid evil, sounds in his heart at the right moment."

CCC 1776

Christian Moral Living

Evan was very close to getting his first "A" in math, a subject he had always found difficult. Two days before his final exam, he saw a copy of the test sitting on his teacher's desk while she was out of the room. Evan was tempted to look at the first few answers so he could go into the test with confidence, even though he knew that was still cheating. But if he knew a few questions in advance, he would have a much better chance of getting that "A"....Evan was torn.

When Carrie joined her friends near the lockers before school, she heard them saying cruel things about a girl who was new to the class. At first, Carrie just listened to their comments, but soon she was joining the conversation, too. It made her feel like she was part of the group. But she also knew these stories about the new girl weren't true. Carrie started feeling guilty. She wanted to be part of the group and if she said something or stopped hanging out they might start talking about her. But how would the new girl feel if she ever found out about the lies her classmates were spreading?

- *What would you do if you were Evan or Carrie?*
- *What would you tell a friend in a similar situation?*

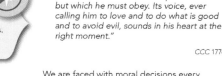

We are faced with moral decisions every day. These decisions, or our choice to not do anything, develop our moral character. Who you are is defined by the decisions you make or don't make when you're asked to choose between right and wrong, between standing up or bowing out. Jesus tells us how important our actions are:

"Everyone who listens to these words of mine and acts on them will be like a wise man who built his house on rock. The rain fell, the floods came, and the winds blew and buffeted the house. But it did not collapse; it had been set solidly on rock. And everyone who listens to these words of mine but does not act on them will be like a fool who built his house on sand. The rain fell, the floods came, and the winds blew and buffeted the house. And it collapsed and was completely ruined."

Matthew 7:24–27

Building your moral house on rock when you're young gives you a strong foundation as you move into adult life. When you choose the right and honest thing consistently, it becomes a habit, and that makes it easier for you to choose the right thing the next time you're faced with a similar option. When we form the habit of choosing honesty, truth, and love, those actions become the ones we default to when facing a problem.

TEENS

CCC 1776–1832

Christian Moral Living

- After reading the introductory section, ask participants to respond to the reflection questions. Then ask if there would be other circumstances under which their response might change.

- Discuss ways we can build or destroy our moral character; ask participants for examples.

Suggested responses include: We build our moral character by choosing what we know is right even if it isn't the popular choice, staying honest even when we might get in trouble, acting out of love for other people, refusing to spread rumors, and so on. We destroy our moral character when we lie or refuse to be accountable for our choices, when we gossip or spread rumors about other people, when we choose to do things we know are wrong, and so on....

- Discuss the relationship between freedom (our free will) and responsibility.

Suggested responses include: Having free will means that we aren't forced to do the right thing. We can choose to do right or wrong and there is no determined path set for us. But we have the responsibility to use that free will in a way that builds up our community and our Church....

Discuss what happens when we act in our own self-interest instead of as followers of Christ.

Suggested responses include: We can degrade our own moral character, we can lead others into bad choices, we present Christianity in a negative light, and so on....

- Emphasize how choosing to not do anything can also be a choice that affects our morality (for example, when we let someone be bullied by not taking part or standing up to stop it).

Our Conscience

- Ask the participants to describe how their consciences have developed as they have matured. You can ask the following questions to prompt discussion: Do they think about moral questions the same way? Do they spend more time asking about circumstances before making a judgment?

- Brainstorm ways you can make time to step back and listen to your conscience when faced with a difficult decision.

Suggested responses include: quiet reflection or contemplation, prayer, journaling, and so on.

- Give participants time to quietly reflect or journal on the reflection questions presented in this section before moving on.

If we fall into the habit of lying, cheating, or deceiving others to get what we want, we are building our houses on sand.

"The education of the conscience is a lifelong task....The education of the conscience guarantees freedom and engenders peace of heart."

CCC 1784

This is where faith can get difficult. Believing in Jesus and understanding the faith are easy in comparison to actually living like Christ. As small children, it's easy to know right from wrong. But when you're faced with more complex moral issues, what's right or wrong may not be as clear, or we know what's right but struggle to follow through with those actions. Plus, the pressure we can feel from the world or friends or family members to make certain decisions makes the task of choosing right or wrong even more difficult.

Because God loves us, we have a free will. Having a **free will** means we have the freedom and power to make choices, to act or not act, to choose how we respond. God won't step in and stop us from making a wrong choice. We have to do our best to discern (make a well-informed decision) what's right and what's wrong; what's the will of God and what's selfish desire.

- How do you make difficult choices?

- Do you ever avoid making choices because you aren't sure what's right or wrong?

Our Conscience

"A well-formed conscience is upright and truthful. It formulates its judgments according to reason, in conformity with the true good willed by the wisdom of the Creator."

CCC 1783

We might have an image of conscience being a little angel and a little devil hovering over each shoulder while telling us what to do or not do. But our conscience is actually a part of who we are. **Conscience** is what enables us to "recognize the moral quality of a concrete act" that we're thinking about doing, in the process of doing, or have already done (CCC 1778). Conscience gives us feelings of peace when we make moral decisions or unrest when we make poor moral choices.

- Write about a time when you felt contentment and joy because you did the right thing.

- Write about a time when you felt uneasy or anxious because you did the wrong thing.

It's important to get into the habit of listening to our conscience, and to be sensitive to how we feel after we have made a difficult choice. Our conscience is subtle. It softly urges us to act as God would want us to act. When we are aware of our consciences and act on what it tells us, we are building that firm foundation written about in Matthew's Gospel.

Unfortunately, we can also get into the habit of ignoring our consciences. We can also miss the quiet voice of our consciences if we don't take time to be quiet and listen. When we're constantly surrounded by the noise of the world, we can miss the gentle voice of conscience inside us. This is where a strong prayer life can help us stay on the right path. Without the quiet and solitude necessary for prayerful reflection and clear thinking, it can be very difficult to discern right from wrong when we are faced with moral decisions.

- What are some ways you can step back from the world and get in touch with your conscience?

Conscience and the Bible

"In the formation of conscience the Word of God is the light for our path; we must assimilate it in faith and prayer and put it into practice. We must also examine our conscience before the Lord's Cross."

CCC 1785

Once we decide to take the time (or make the time) to come to know God's will, we can begin our search with sacred Scripture. Jesus promises us, "Whoever loves me will keep my word, and my Father will love him, and we will come to him and make our dwelling with him" (John 14:23). These are wonderfully reassuring words. They tell us that if we make Jesus the center of our lives and use his words and actions as our guide, we will know the best way to live. We will not be perfect. We'll fail sometimes and make bad choices, but Jesus won't give up on us. He dwells within us and will work to bring us back on track.

The moral teaching of Jesus includes understanding and obeying the **commandments** of the Old Testament. The Ten Commandments were accepted by the Jews in Jesus' time as God's will. They were given to Moses on Mount Sinai (Exodus 20:1–21; Deuteronomy 5:1–21). They have remained the standards of morality for generations.

After the Israelites escaped from slavery in Egypt, God gave them the commandments to keep them from falling into a worse form of slavery—slavery to sin. When we lie, steal, or take another's life, we can't be truly free. We can't experience full human joy. The great value of the commandments can be seen if we ask ourselves the simple question, "What would the world be like tomorrow if everyone kept the Ten Commandments?"

- *How do you think the world would be different if everyone followed the Ten Commandments?*

The Moral Teachings of Jesus

[Jesus said] "But what comes out of a person, that is what defiles. From within people, from their hearts, come evil thoughts, unchastity, theft, murder, adultery, greed, malice, deceit, licentiousness, envy, blasphemy, arrogance, folly."

Mark 7:20–22

Jesus did more than affirm the Ten Commandments. He challenged us to aim for an even higher standard—a morality based on love. Jesus questioned old beliefs that allowed hatred and revenge. He told us it was not enough to follow the law if our hearts were full of anger and hatred.

Jesus was urging us to move beyond legalism—obeying a list of laws—to a morality that truly fosters love. When we choose to obey the speed limits, we should do so out of respect for the safety and well-being of others—not simply because it's the law and we don't want a ticket. When we choose to avoid saying something untrue about another person, we should be motivated by our love and respect for the children of God—not just the need to obey the Ten Commandments.

Conscience and the Church

Catholics believe that we have another resource to help us form good consciences—the teachings of the Church. Jesus is present in his Church and has given its leaders the authority to speak and act in his name. New Testament Christians looked to their leaders for guidance in moral questions, like when the Corinthians wrote to Paul for advice (1 Corinthians 7:1). All New Testament letters offered moral guidance, and some gave rules of conduct in matters of Church organization, relationships with one another, and daily life.

Since then, the Catholic Church has provided moral leadership for its members through laws and instruction from pastors, bishops, and popes. Church leaders strive to understand and teach how the Gospel applies to modern life.

The Moral Teachings of Jesus

- Emphasize that Jesus takes the Ten Commandments a step further when he gives the two great commandments (in today's reading)—both based on love of God and neighbor rather than simply following the letter of the law. Read section 1778 in the *Catechism* and ask participants to reflect on what it says.

Conscience and the Church

- Emphasize for participants that following the teachings of the Church is not about simply not sinning or finding a loophole in a teaching we, personally, find difficult to accept. The ultimate goal of our lives as Christians, and the teachings of the Church, is to live more like Christ on earth and to prepare for eternal life in heaven. This means there will be times we have to let go of our personal opinions and embrace Church teachings—even if that process is painful or confusing for a time.

- If participants have additional questions or you'd like to spend more time covering this topic, see CCC 143–152, which talks about a free submission to the whole truth revealed by God, and CCC 85–95, which discusses in more detail the Magisterium of the Church and our duty to adhere to its teachings and interpretations of the law as inspired by the Holy Spirit.

- Participants may have questions about whether or not they can dissent from Church teachings because they feel the Church is wrong about a particular point. It is important to distinguish between the three levels of Church teaching: dogma, definitive doctrine, and authoritative doctrine. We cannot dissent Church dogma or definitive doctrine without separating from the Church. While it is possible to dissent from authoritative doctrine, that dissent must still come from a place of submission of will and intellect to God and the Church. This kind of dissent is only possible in very rare circumstances.

- Refer to the *Dogmatic Constitution on the Church* (*Lumen Gentium*), 25. Dissent is possible, but only if a person has sufficient expertise to study the matter thoroughly and has discovered important reasons, that the person believes were unknown to the pope, that would cause him to alter his decision. If such be the case, the person may suspend his or her assent until the pope has made a final decision.

- You may also refer to Pope St. John Paul II's apostolic letter *Motu Proprio Ad Tuendam Fidem* and the Congregation for the Doctrine of the Faith's "Doctrinal Commentary on the Concluding Formula of the Professio Fidei."

- As you conclude the lesson, discuss tools that human beings have to help them make good moral choices.

Suggested responses include: the Bible, the teachings of Jesus, the teachings of the Church, the influence of family, the influence of responsible friends, the virtues and gifts of the Spirit [CCC 1828, 1830]).

C13

Forming Your Conscience

With a partner, make up a scenario that would require you to make a difficult choice. Work through steps one through four under "Forming Your Conscience" and come up with a way to handle that scenario. Share with the rest of the group. *(An example follows.)*

Scenario: You're at the store and, after reviewing your receipt, you notice the cashier didn't ring up one of your items but included it in your bag. Do you go back and pay for the item or consider it a bonus and do nothing?

1. *After prayerful reflection, you might begin to think that leaving without paying for an item, even if you had every intention to, is still taking something you didn't pay for.*

2. *The Ten Commandments say stealing is wrong, but is this really exactly the same as stealing? Following the spirit of this commandment, however, would require you to go back and pay.*

3. *Church teachings would tell you that taking something that doesn't belong to you, no matter how you got it, isn't the moral thing to do. It would also tell you that you should respect the cashier and do what you can to help correct the mistake.*

4. *Solution: While you haven't actually done anything wrong yet, keeping the item knowing you didn't pay for it and that you haven't attempted to make things right would be the immoral choice. You should return to the store, explain the situation, and pay for the item.*

Catholics trust that Church leaders continue to be guided by the Holy Spirit. As we seek to make good moral choices, it's important to know the moral teachings of the Church and, more importantly, to understand the reasons behind these teachings. The *Catechism of the Catholic Church* is a great place to start if you have questions on Church teaching, but your sponsor or parish priest can be great resources, too.

Forming Your Conscience

When we are faced with moral decisions, there are several steps we can take to make sure our consciences are well-formed:

1. Take the time or make the time for prayerful reflection. Make sure you can hear the small voice within.

2. Know and understand the Ten Commandments, and then ask yourself, "What would be the morally right thing to do?"

3. Know and understand the teachings of the Church. If a Church teaching is confusing, don't be afraid to discuss that issue with a priest or well-informed Catholic.

4. If you make a mistake, seek forgiveness and grow from what you've learned.

With a partner, make up a scenario that would require you to make a difficult choice.

Work through steps 1 to 4 under "Forming Your Conscience" and come up with a way to handle that scenario. Share with the rest of the group.

Recall a time when you did something wrong that you later regretted.

If you were faced with that situation again, how would you respond?

Journey of Faith for Teens: Catechumenate, C13 (826290)
Imprimi Potest: Stephen T. Rehrauer, CSsR, Provincial, Denver Province, the Redemptorists.
Imprimatur: "In accordance with CIC 827, permission to publish has been granted on March 29, 2016, by the Most Reverend Edward M. Rice, Auxiliary Bishop, Archdiocese of St. Louis. Permission to publish is an indication that nothing contrary to Church teaching is contained in this work. It does not imply any endorsement of the opinions expressed in the publication, nor is any liability assumed by this permission."
Journey of Faith © 1993, 2005, 2016 Liguori Publications, Liguori, MO 63057. To order, visit Liguori.org or call 800-325-9521. Liguori Publications, a nonprofit corporation, is an apostolate of the Redemptorists. To learn more about the Redemptorists, visit Redemptorists.com. All rights reserved. No part of this publication may be reproduced, distributed, stored, transmitted, or posted in any form by any means without prior written permission. Text: Adapted from *Journey of Faith for Adults* © 2000 Liguori Publications. Editors of 2016 edition: Theresa Nienaber and Pat Fosarelli, MD, DMin. Design: Lorena Mitre Jimenez. Unless noted, Scripture texts in this work are taken from *New American Bible*, revised edition. © 2010, 1991, 1986, 1970 Confraternity of Christian Doctrine, Washington, D.C., and are used by permission of the copyright owner. All Rights Reserved. No part of *New American Bible* may be reproduced in any form without permission in writing from the copyright owner. Excerpts from English translation of the *Catechism of the Catholic Church* for the United States of America © 1994 United States Catholic Conference, Inc. —*Libreria Editrice Vaticana*; English translation of the *Catechism of the Catholic Church, Modifications from the Editio Typica* © 1997 United States Catholic Conference, Inc. —*Libreria Editrice Vaticana.* Compliant with *The Roman Missal, Third Edition.*
Printed in the United States of America. 20 19 18 17 16 / 5 4 3 2 1. Third Edition.

Liguori PUBLICATIONS
A Redemptorist Ministry

Journaling

Recall a time when you did something wrong that you later regretted. If you were faced with that situation again, how would you respond?

Closing Prayer

Dim the lights and have the participants gather in comfortable positions. Keep the candle lit. Play a recording of "Restless" as a closing prayer.

Looking Ahead

Before next class, ask participants to think of some moral issues we struggle with today that didn't exist for the early Church. Where can we look for guidance on these issues? Where can we find guidance on modern-day issues?

C14: The Dignity of Life

Catechism: 1807, 2401–2449

Objectives

- Reflect on the universal dignity of human life.
- Recognize protection of life as a matter of justice.
- Apply the concepts of dignity, justice, and the rights to social justice.
- Identify forms of discrimination and oppression.

Leader Meditation

Luke 10:25–37

Thank God for the people in your life who have been Good Samaritans to you. Think about simple, everyday ways that you can be a Good Samaritan to others.

Leader Preparation

- Read the lesson, this lesson plan, the Scripture passage, and the *Catechism* sections.
- Familiarize yourself with any world or national current events that center on the issues of economic or social justice; use these events as examples.
- Be familiar with the vocabulary terms for this lesson: economy, prejudice. Definitions are provided in this guide's glossary.

Welcome

Greet participants as they arrive. Check for supplies and immediate needs. Solicit questions or comments about the previous session and/or share new information and findings. Begin promptly.

Opening Scripture

Luke 10:25–37

Ask a volunteer to light the candle and read aloud. Ask the participants to give examples of when someone took time from a busy life to help them in some way. Before beginning your discussion of the lesson handout, discuss with participants ***how acts of charity and kindness, no matter how small, affect human dignity.***

> Justice is the moral virtue that consists in the constant and firm will to give [our] due to God and neighbor....The just man, often mentioned in the Sacred Scriptures, is distinguished by habitual right thinking and the uprightness of his conduct toward his neighbor. *CCC 1807*

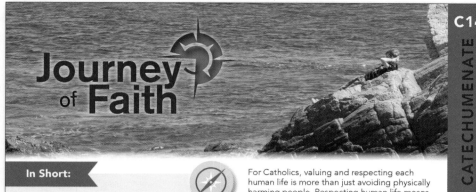

Journey of Faith

In Short:

- The dignity of life is universal.
- Christians are called to protect life.
- Christians are called to support dignity, justice, and rights for all.

The Dignity of Life

In a recent experiment, members of half of a freshman class were asked to wear white collars for the day. They were told that they were inferior to their classmates who didn't have to wear the white collars. The "white collars" were forced to do more work in class and were graded more harshly. They were forced to go to lunch last, after all the good choices were gone. Teachers treated them as less intelligent. Before long, the students wearing white collars began to actually feel inferior. More surprisingly, they didn't do as well on their schoolwork as they normally would have.

The following day, the other half of the class wore the white collars, and they experienced the same feelings of inferiority.

- *What does this experiment tell you about how you treat others?*
- *Have you ever been influenced (positively or negatively) by someone else's opinion of you?*

For Catholics, valuing and respecting each human life is more than just avoiding physically harming people. Respecting human life means working to make sure that every person can live with dignity. Living with dignity means living in a way that brings honor and respect to others and yourself. The teachings of Christ demand that we take a stand against anything in society that denies people's rights and dignity.

> "The Church receives from the Gospel the full revelation of the truth about man. The Church bears witness to man, in the name of Christ, to the dignity of mankind and mankind's vocation to the communion of persons. She teaches him the demands of justice and peace in conformity with divine wisdom."
>
> CCC 2419

Economic Justice

In *Economic Justice for All: Catholic Social Teaching and the U.S. Economy*, the U.S. Catholic bishops wrote that every perspective on economic life must be shaped by three questions:

- What does the economy do for people?
- What does it do to people?
- And how do people participate in it?

A country's **economy** is its system for producing, distributing, and consuming wealth, usually in the form of goods and money. The bishops insist that economic decisions have moral consequences because they directly affect the human person by either enhancing or destroying human dignity.

CCC 1807; 2401–2449

The Dignity of Life

- Discuss the social experiment involving the white collars. Ask participants for examples of times when society has made others feel inferior because they were part of a specific group.

  Suggested responses include: the treatment of black Americans throughout American history or the wearing of the yellow star by Jews in Nazi Europe.

- Ask participants if they've ever felt differently about themselves because of someone else's opinion of them (this can be positive or negative).

- If time allows, discuss the "Think About" questions as a group, or give participants time to write their responses in their journal. If you're short on time, have participants think about their responses and then move on to a discussion of the reflection question.

- As you go through each section, keep a running list of all the ways participants can help where they are now. If you can, make the list available to participants outside of class.

Economic Justice

Suggested responses to the reflection question include: Donating unused or slightly used clothing and other items, starting a fund-raiser for a specific Catholic charity or organization in your area that serves the poor, by treating everyone you meet with the same respect regardless of where you meet them, by making eye contact with and acknowledging the poor or homeless near you, and so on....

Equality: One Creator, One Destiny

Suggested responses to the reflection question include: Choosing not to believe rumors or gossip, getting to know those you'd otherwise write off based on appearances or stereotypes, acting the same way toward people when you're being watched and when you're not, and so on....

At the time of the bishops' letter (1986), the U.S. economy was experiencing tremendous productivity, yet thirty-three million people remained poor. The bishops wrote their letter not to condemn the United States or its wealthy citizens but to urge Catholics and other citizens to face the reality of poverty.

"Only, we were to be mindful of the poor, which is the very thing I was eager to do."

Galatians 2:10

True charity goes beyond just ending misery or alleviating needs. It demands genuine love for the person. We respect and care about others because they, like us, are children of God.

The U.S. bishops named ways that society can work toward building the dignity of the poor. Many of these things don't require you to have power or money yourself. You can further the mission of caring for the poor in simple ways.

Think about:

- How do you treat the students in your class who don't have the money to buy the "right" clothes or electronics?

- Do you actively participate in school, church, and community programs that serve the needs of the poor?

- Do you educate yourself about the real causes of poverty, rather than assuming stereotypes are accurate?

- Do you see the suffering Christ in the faces of the poor?

- *What are some ways you can help the poor in your area?*

Equality: One Creator, One Destiny

"...When [the Church] fulfills her mission of proclaiming the Gospel, she bears witness to man, in the name of Christ, to his dignity and his vocation to the communion of persons."

CCC 2419

All people—regardless of their race, religion, gender, national origin, sexual preference, political party, or language—must be treated with equal dignity. All people have been created by God and are called to spend eternity with God in heaven.

While most of us agree with such statements about equality, we have all also been exposed to prejudice toward one group or another. **Prejudice** is an unfavorable judgment or opinion about someone that is formed without knowing the facts or in spite of the facts. Prejudice is often rooted in fear. It is almost always the product of ignorance.

Today the bishops challenge us to work toward abolishing all forms of prejudice through our attitudes and actions in our schools, families, organizations, athletic groups, and circles of friends.

The Second Vatican Council noted that "every type of discrimination, whether social or cultural, whether based on sex, race, color, social condition, language, or religion, is to be overcome...as contrary to God's intent....Such is the case of the woman who is denied the right and freedom to choose a husband, to embrace a state of life, or to acquire an education or cultural benefits equal to those recognized for men" (Constitution on the Church [Lumen Gentium], 29).

Think about:

- Do you form opinions of people when you first meet them based on money or how they look?

- Have you ever viewed people as being more or less intelligent based on their gender or ethnicity?

- Do you treat people differently depending on who else is around?

- Do you strive to see how all people contribute to the body of Christ?

- *How can you continue to put the dignity of others first in your relationships?*

The Stewardship of Creation

"God looked at everything he had made, and found it very good. Evening came, and morning followed—the sixth day."

Genesis 1:31

Christian concern for the environment begins with understanding the natural world as God's gift to us. Our Christian tradition teaches us that we must exercise responsible stewardship. We must treasure the gift of creation through the wise use of natural resources and by working to preserve the earth.

In his writing, *On Social Concerns*, Pope St. John Paul II said animals, plants, and natural things cannot be used "simply as one wishes, according to one's own economic needs. On the contrary, one must take into account the nature of each being and of its mutual connection in an ordered system..." More recently in *Laudato Si'*, Pope Francis wrote, "The harmony between the Creator, humanity, and creation as a whole was disrupted by our presuming to take the place of God...We are not God. The earth was here before us, and it has been given to us" (66–67). Care for creation is an area where you can really make a difference.

Think about:
- Do I do everything I can to keep the natural world around me clean and unspoiled?
- Do I always dispose of my trash properly?
- Do I take the time to pick up trash that others have carelessly left?
- Do I influence my peers to recycle?
- Do I educate myself about products that are harmful to the environment and then seek to avoid them?
- Do I do positive things for my little corner of the world, such as planting trees and gardens?

- What are some other ways you can have a positive effect on the world around you?

The Work of the World

In our society, work is commonly considered something we do so we can have the money to do what we really want. Church teaching offers a far richer perspective on the meaning and value of work for humanity. Pope St. John Paul II tells us, "Life is built up every day from work, from work it derives its specific dignity" (*On Human Work* [*Laborem exercens*], 1). The world of work needs our attention because it can be either a way to build up the dignity of human beings or destroy it.

The Church warns that human labor should never be thought of as just another resource in the production process, like money, technology, or raw materials. No matter what work we do, we are human beings who must be treated with respect and paid a fair wage. Work should never be degrading.

The U.S. Catholic bishops wrote, "Work is not only for oneself. It is for one's family, for the nation, and indeed for the benefit of the entire human family" (Economic Justice for All). When we find ourselves in the workplace, whether it's a part-time job or our future career, it's important to consider the moral significance of our choice. We must consider not only our personal interests, talents, and needs but also the effect our work will have on the world as a whole.

Think about:
- How can I make the world a better place through my work?
- Do I consistently put my best effort behind what I do?
- Do I treat all my coworkers with respect, even when I disagree with them?
- When I go out to a restaurant or a store, do I treat the people serving me with dignity and respect?

- What are some ways you can bring the love of Christ into your work, whether it's a school project, part-time job, or volunteer position?

The Stewardship of Creation

Suggested responses to the reflection question include: Treating the natural world with the respect due to God's creation, recycling when you can and encouraging others to do the same, going outside and enjoying time in nature, participating in community gardening projects, and so on....

The Work of the World

Suggested responses to the reflection question include: viewing every project or assignment as worthy of your time, handling disagreements respectfully and staying open to other's opinions and contributions, treating the work of others with respect, and more....

- As you conclude the lesson, emphasize that living justly is a way of life, a habit that we must begin early in our lives and practice daily. Encourage participants to go back to the list you created in class or their own notes and actually do some of the actions suggested.

As a group, read this anecdote and answer the questions:

It has been said that Christopher Wren, a great English architect, walked unrecognized among workers building St. Paul's Cathedral in London. "What are you doing?" he asked one of the workers, and the man replied, "I am cutting a piece of stone." As he went on he asked the same question to another man, who replied, "I am earning five shilling two pence a day." To a third he asked the same and the man answered, "I am helping to build a cathedral."

How does the response of each man show his attitude toward his work?

Suggested responses include: The first man looks only at his work and not the effect it has on the project, the second man looks only at what he's being paid, the third man sees the full scope of his work.

How does the response of the third man reflect the teaching of the Catholic Church?

Suggested responses include: The third response shows the true value of each role and each assignment we receive, and how even small parts influence the larger outcome of our work—and God's kingdom.

How is this point of view related to the dignity of life?

Suggested responses include: It shows there is dignity in all work, even if it doesn't feel like we're making progress or building something important, it shows that our work should be more to us than just a paycheck or a grade, and more.

Journey of Faith for Teens: Catechumenate, C14 (826290)
Imprimi Potest: Stephen T. Rehrauer, CSsR, Provincial, Denver Province, the Redemptorists.
Imprimatur: "In accordance with CIC 827, permission to publish has been granted on March 29, 2016, by the Most Reverend Edward M. Rice, Auxiliary Bishop, Archdiocese of St. Louis. Permission to publish is an indication that nothing contrary to Church teaching is contained in this work. It does not imply any endorsement of the opinions expressed in the publication; nor is any liability assumed by this permission."
Journey of Faith © 1993, 2005, 2016 Liguori Publications, Liguori, MO 63057. To order, visit Liguori.org or call 800-325-9521. Liguori Publications, a nonprofit corporation, is an apostolate of the Redemptorists. To learn more about the Redemptorists, visit Redemptorists.com. All rights reserved. No part of this publication may be reproduced, distributed, stored, transmitted, or posted in any form by any means without prior written permission. Text: Adapted from Journey of Faith for Adults © 2000 Liguori Publications. Editors of 2016 edition: Theresa Nienaber and Pat Fosarelli, MD, DMin. Design: Lorena Mitre Jimenez. Unless noted, Scripture texts in this work are taken from New American Bible, revised edition © 2010, 1991, 1986, 1970 Confraternity of Christian Doctrine, Washington, D.C., and are used by permission of the copyright owner. All Rights Reserved. No part of New American Bible may be reproduced in any form without permission in writing from the copyright owner. Excerpts from English translation of the Catechism of the Catholic Church for the United States of America © 1994 United States Catholic Conference, Inc. —Libreria Editrice Vaticana; English translation of the Catechism of the Catholic Church: Modifications from the Editio Typica © 1997 United States Catholic Conference, Inc. —Libreria Editrice Vaticana. Excerpts from Vatican documents © 2016 Libreria Editrice Vaticana and are used with permission. Compliant with The Roman Missal, Third Edition.
Printed in the United States of America. 20 19 18 17 16 / 5 4 3 2 1. Third Edition.

Journaling

Think about areas in your school, neighborhood, or community where you see inequalities. Then try to come up with one small way you can work to improve the situation.

Closing Prayer

After mentioning any special intentions, ask for a volunteer to read Matthew 5:43–48 as a closing prayer. Here, Jesus asks that we treat everyone, even our enemies, with justice. Conclude by praying the Lord's Prayer together.

Take-home

Tomorrow or some other day in the next week, ask participants to pay special attention to the people around them at school, at work, or in their neighborhoods, and then go out of their way to do something kind for them as an acknowledgment of their dignity.

C15: A Consistent Ethic of Life

Catechism: 1807, 2401–2449

Objectives

- Name contemporary issues that threaten human life, such as abortion, war, euthanasia, capital punishment, and some reproductive technologies.
- Cite examples of "intrinsic moral evil."
- Discuss how Catholics can defend life with great strength and virtue.

Leader Meditation

Genesis 1:24–31

In this passage, the ancient writers speak of God as the author of all life. They proclaim that everything God made is sacred, beautiful, and good. Reflect on the power—and responsibility—inherent in this message.

Leader Preparation

- Read the lesson, this lesson plan, the Scripture passage, and the *Catechism* sections.
- Consider having newspapers, magazines, or internet access for participants to research current world events.
- Be familiar with the vocabulary terms for this lesson: consistent life ethic, abortion, euthanasia, capital punishment. Definitions are provided in this guide's glossary.

Welcome

Greet participants as they arrive. Check for supplies and immediate needs. Solicit questions or comments about the previous session and/or share new information and findings. Begin promptly.

Opening Scripture

Genesis 1:24–31

Ask for a volunteer to light the candle and read aloud. Following the reading, reflect on what important truth the author, inspired by the Holy Spirit, was trying to convey. Then, before beginning your discussion of the lesson handout, ask participants: ***What does Genesis tell us about the value of all life, especially human life, in the eyes of God?***

> Human life is sacred because from its beginning it involves the creative action of God and it remains forever in a special relationship with the Creator, who is its sole end. God alone is the Lord of life from its beginning until its end. *CCC 2258*

Journey of Faith

In Short:

- Catholics should be aware of contemporary issues threaten human life.
- Some actions are intrinsic moral evils.
- Catholics should always work to defend life.

A Consistent Ethic of Life

A Story of Life

In the year 1287, a little girl was born into a noble Italian family. Margaret's family didn't want her. She had a humpback, one leg was shorter than the other, her head was an unusual shape, and she was blind.

BL. MARGARET OF CASTELLO OP

Her parents told people Margaret died at birth and banished her from the main rooms of their castle. Afraid that her identity might be revealed, her parents walled her into a tiny room in a forest chapel. Margaret didn't lose heart. With the help of the chapel priest, she learned how to turn her prison into a place of quiet contemplation.

Later, Margaret's parents took her to a city known for healing miracles, but when she wasn't miraculously cured they abandoned her at the church. Again, Margaret did not despair. Here she began giving her love and compassion to the poor of the city. This was the beginning of her remarkable ministry to the poor and the needy. Eventually she became a Third Order Dominican,

a lay member of the Dominican order. Her own life allowed her to understand the pain and suffering of others. Her faith and courage transformed her anguish into compassion. Today she is known by the Church as Blessed Margaret of Castello.

"Choose life, then, that you and your descendents may live, by loving the LORD, your God, obeying his voice, and holding fast to him."

Deuteronomy 30:19–20

In 1983, Joseph Cardinal Bernardin called on U.S. Catholics to adopt what is called a **consistent life ethic**. This means we consider all human life sacred. For Catholics, life begins at the moment of conception until natural death. This includes the unborn, the elderly, the dying, the suffering, the imprisoned, and those with disabilities or mental illness. A consistent life ethic means there are no exceptions. Every human life is sacred.

Standing for a consistent life ethic means opposing **intrinsic moral evils**, actions that are always morally wrong, that threaten or demean human life, such as abortion or euthanasia. This also means considering **morally problematic** actions that may be justified but only in very specific instances, like war or capital punishment within the teaching and instruction of the Church.

Cardinal Bernardin said that a consistent life ethic would also include equally strong support for positive social programs that honor and respect life, from feeding the hungry and housing the homeless to helping the elderly and immigrants. Possessing a truly consistent life ethic is more difficult than it sounds and requires we not only believe but act on our beliefs.

CCC 1807, 2401–2449

A Consistent Ethic of Life

- After reading the introduction, ask the participants for reactions. What lesson does this story have for us? What does it teach us about how we are called to value life?

Suggested responses include: it gives us an example of what it means to live and practice a consistent ethic of life and what it means to embrace the intrinsic human dignity of all.

- Ask participants to explain the consistent ethic of life in their own words.

- As participants discuss the consistent ethic of life, take this opportunity to emphasize that as Catholics having a consistent ethic of life requires two things. The first is that we acknowledge and actively treat every threat to the dignity of human life. The second, that we give each threat its proper weight by recognizing some involve an intrinsically evil act (such as abortion or euthanasia) while others involve morally problematic acts (such as war or capital punishment).

- Discuss why it's important Catholics have a united view of how life should be valued and treated, and how this view might differ from how society views life.

Suggested responses include: Catholics need to be united because the Catholic view isn't always the rest of the world's view; if we're going to change the way people view life, we need to present a consistent stance; the world sometimes views the value of a life based on what it can do, what it looks like, or what it can do for the world....

Abortion and the Unique Preciousness of Life

- As you discuss this section, emphasize that a consistent life ethic requires us to treat the life of the unborn child and the life of the mother with equal dignity.

- As a group or individually, ask participants to list ways they see parishioners actively involved in pro-life work.

War and the Rights of the Innocent

- If you have time, pause after your discussion of war to research some current events where a consistent life ethic is needed (or already in action). Create a list as a group, or have participants respond to these reflection questions on their own in their journals.

- This section may also be a good time to bring up Church teaching on intrinsic moral evils and morally problematic choices. An intrinsic moral evil is an action that is always morally wrong (abortion, euthanasia, embryonic stem-cell research, and others). Morally problematic actions are actions that may be justified, but only in very specific instances (like war or capital punishment).

> "Give to everyone who asks of you, and from the one who takes what is yours do not demand it back. Do to others as you would have them do to you."
>
> *Luke 6:30–31*

- Can you think of other examples of value blindness?
- How can we work to overcome these kinds of perceptions?

Abortion and the Unique Preciousness of Life

> "Human life must be respected and protected absolutely from the moment of conception. From the first moment of conception. From the first moment of his existence, a human being must be recognized as having the rights of a person—among which is the inviolable right of every innocent being to life."
>
> *CCC 2270*

Abortion, the killing of an unborn child, is easily recognizable as a terrible evil because it destroys the most innocent and fragile form of human life. However, the issue of abortion can seem more complicated when we consider a young mother who isn't prepared, a family already in dire poverty, and the other fears and anxieties that can drive a woman to an abortion.

Catholic moral tradition not only asks us to protect the life of every unborn child but also requires we work to help ease the burden of the mother facing an unplanned pregnancy. We can help families bear these burdens by supporting or volunteering with an organization that provides abortion alternatives alongside financial and emotional supports.

- What are some ways you see members of your parish community supporting the pro-life movement?

War and the Rights of the Innocent

> "Peace is not merely the absence of war, and it is not limited to maintaining a balance of powers between adversaries. Peace cannot be attained on earth without safeguarding the goods of persons, free communication among men, respect for the dignity of persons and peoples, and the assiduous practice of fraternity."
>
> *CCC 2304*

God created us to live in peace and harmony. The creation story in Genesis describes God's plan for our peaceful existence. Every human being has the right to live his or her life without fear of aggression. While Catholic teaching has always allowed for war in defense of one's country, the nature of modern war has greatly increased our need to work for peace in all circumstances. Modern warfare now affects the lives of thousands of innocent people.

The Church tells us that our respect for human life—including the lives of the citizens of countries with unjust or aggressive governments—makes it extremely important that we work for peace through meaningful, sincere negotiation and discussion. If we wish to uphold the values of Jesus, modern war can never be the way to lasting peace.

- List current world events where a consistent life ethic is needed.
- List current world events where a consistent life ethic is present.

Euthanasia and Life's Sacredness

> "Those whose lives are diminished or weakened deserve special respect. Sick or handicapped persons should be helped to lead lives as normal as possible. Whatever its motives and means, direct euthanasia consists in putting an end to the lives of handicapped, sick, or dying persons. It is morally unacceptable."
>
> *CCC 2276–2277*

Euthanasia and Life's Sacredness

- Discuss with participants how allowing God to end life in his time preserves the dignity of life and death more so than euthanasia. If time allows, you may want to review the *Catechism* section on euthanasia (2276–2279) to help with this discussion.

Many sincere Christians have become confused about **euthanasia** or physician-assisted suicide (deliberately ending someone's life) in recent times for two main reasons:

First, modern medical science has made it possible for many people who once would have died to continue living under conditions that are extremely burdensome to them or to those who care for them.

Second, pro-euthanasia organizations attempt to make us believe that we have a right to die when physical or mental pain becomes more than we believe we can bear. From their viewpoint, providing "death with dignity" is a noble duty for caregivers.

This stance blinds us to several things. We begin to believe that life's painful moments are all strikes against what should be a pain-free and happy life. We forget that pain and difficulties are part of human life and that we can grow tremendously from them. We see only two options for those sick and suffering, an existence filled with tremendous pain or death. In reality, today's hospice programs specialize in caring for people who are dealing with incurable diseases or certain death. Hospice caregivers specialize in the management of pain, both physical and emotional. They work with the patient and the patient's family, supporting them with necessary pain medications, counseling, and medical information.

The Catholic Church teaches that life is sacred, even in its final phases on earth, but that doesn't mean we must cling to life on earth by all extraordinary means when death is likely. The deliberate killing of the sick or disabled is contrary to God's law.

On the other hand, we don't need to prolong a person's life with extraordinary technology when there is no hope of recovery. Human beings should be allowed to die a natural death. The Church recognizes God as the author of every human life. It also recognizes God as the one who determines when every human life will end its earthly existence.

- How does allowing God to determine when life ends preserve the dignity of life?

?

Capital Punishment or Life Imprisonment

"If, however, non-lethal means are sufficient to defend and protect people's safety from the aggressor, authority will limit itself to such means, as these are more in keeping with the concrete conditions of the common good and more in conformity with the dignity of the human person."

CCC 2267

Capital punishment, the death penalty, is a difficult issue. Even those who consider themselves pro-life disagree with each other over capital punishment. Those opposing capital punishment argue that all killing is wrong, even the killing of a hardened criminal. Those who believe that capital punishment is sometimes justified say that abortion is absolutely different from the punishment of those who have deliberately taken the lives of others. Both sides make compelling arguments.

The Catholic Church has always tried to balance justice and mercy in regard to the treatment of those who commit murder. The U.S. bishops have chosen to place the stress on witnessing to the value of every human life, no matter how guilty the individual may be, by voting against support for state laws allowing capital punishment. The bishops support the use and enforcement of life imprisonment so that the criminal can no longer be a threat to society.

But perhaps most importantly, the U.S. bishops are seeking to uphold a consistent life ethic even under the most difficult of circumstances. Christ consistently regarded all life as precious and valuable. He saw every life as being created in the image and likeness of God. The Catholic Church challenges us to do the same.

Capital Punishment or Life Imprisonment

- Talk about why abortion, capital punishment, euthanasia, and unjust wars do not comply with a consistent life ethic, even though they may seem like the answer at the time.

A Consistent Ethic of Life

Pick one of the three issues below and answer the following questions.

Suggested responses include:

What reasons do people give for it?

Capital punishment: *It prevents criminals from ever committing another crime.*

Euthanasia: *Prolonged terminal suffering is unjust if someone is aware of their options and chooses assisted suicide.*

Abortion: *A woman has the right to choose what happens in her own body, some children may be born into poverty or extreme suffering.*

Against it?

Capital punishment: *Life in prison is punishment enough; there are other ways to prevent someone from committing crimes.*

Euthanasia: *Suffering can be an opportunity for spiritual graces; even the lives of the terminally ill have value.*

Abortion: *The child has a right to life; options other than abortion exist to help alleviate suffering of both the child and mother.*

CATECHUMENATE

JOURNEY OF FAITH

Pick one of the three issues below and answer the following questions:

—What reasons do people give for it?

—Against it?

—What does the Church teach?

(1) Capital punishment (2) Euthanasia (3) Abortion

Being pro-life doesn't just mean participating in these issues on a large or political scale. We can show our respect for life in small, everyday actions.

List some ways you can become more pro-life or ways you can show others their lives have value.

Journey of Faith for Teens: Catechumenate, C15 (826290)
Imprimi Potest: Stephen T. Rehrauer, CSsR, Provincial, Denver Province, the Redemptorists.
Imprimatur: "In accordance with CIC 827, permission to publish has been granted on March 23, 2016, by the Most Reverend Edward M. Rice, Auxiliary Bishop, Archdiocese of St. Louis. Permission to publish is an indication that nothing contrary to Church teaching is contained in this work. It does not imply any endorsement of the opinions expressed in the publication, nor is any liability assumed by this permission."
Journey of Faith © 2000, 2016 Liguori Publications, Liguori, MO 63057. To order, visit Liguori.org or call 800-325-9521. Liguori Publications, a nonprofit corporation, is an apostolate of the Redemptorists. To learn more about the Redemptorists, visit Redemptorists.com. All rights reserved. No part of this publication may be reproduced, distributed, stored, transmitted, or posted in any form by any means without prior written permission.
Text: Adapted from *Journey of Faith* © 2000 Liguori Publications. Editors of 2016 *Journey of Faith*: Theresa Nienaber and Pat Fosarelli, MD, DMin. Design: Lorena Mitre Jimenez. Images: Shutterstock and Wikimedia Commons: Judgefloro.
Unless noted, Scripture texts in this work are taken from *New American Bible, revised edition* © 2010, 1991, 1986, 1970 Confraternity of Christian Doctrine, Washington, D.C., and are used by permission of the copyright owner. All Rights Reserved. No part of *New American Bible* may be reproduced in any form without permission in writing from the copyright owner. Excerpts from English translation of the *Catechism of the Catholic Church for the United States of America* © 1994 United States Catholic Conference, Inc. —Libreria Editrice Vaticana; English translation of the *Catechism of the Catholic Church: Modifications from the Editio Typica* © 1997 United States Catholic Conference, Inc. —Libreria Editrice Vaticana. Compliant with *The Roman Missal, Third Edition*.
Printed in the United States of America. 20 19 18 17 16 / 5 4 3 2 1. Third Edition.

LIGUORI
PUBLICATIONS
A Redemptorist Ministry

What does the Church teach?

Capital punishment: *The death penalty can only be used if it's the only way to defend innocent human lives (CCC 2267).*

Euthanasia: *The human lives of the terminally ill, sick, or diminished still have value, murder in the guise of mercy is still contrary to the dignity of the human person and disrespectful to God (CCC 2276–2279).*

Abortion: *Human life must be protected from the moment of conception, all human beings have an inviolable right to life, it is the role of the Christian to defend and speak out for those who cannot defend or speak out for themselves (CCC 2270–2275).*

Journaling

Being pro-life doesn't just mean participating in these issues on a large or political scale. We can show our respect for life in small, everyday actions. List some ways you can become more pro-life or ways you can show others their lives have value.

Closing Prayer

Ask the participants to first bring to mind any special intentions—especially for the sick, dying, and unborn. Thank God for the gift of life. Conclude with this excerpt from Bishop Robert Baker's pro-life prayer.

Lord God,...You are the Protector and Defender of the lives of the innocent unborn...Change the hearts of those who compromise the call to protect and defend life. Bring our nation to the values that have made us a great nation, a society that upholds the values of life, liberty, and the pursuit of happiness for all. Amen.

Looking Ahead

The way we think about life as Catholics influences the way we live our lives and interact with our community. Before next class, ask participants to think about some of the ways Catholics live out this consistent ethic of life through service to the community.

C16: Social Justice

Catechism: 1928–1942

Objectives

- Recognize that Church teachings on social justice are founded in Christ and advancing to meet the needs of a changing society.
- Explore papal and Vatican documents on social justice.
- Identify the seven themes of Catholic social teaching.
- Determine ways to promote justice and advocate for the poor and vulnerable.

Leader Meditation

Luke 16:19–31

When have you felt like Lazarus and who cared for you? How can you respond to those like Lazarus in your world?

Leader Preparation

- Read the lesson, this lesson plan, the Scripture passage, and the *Catechism* sections.

Welcome

Greet participants as they arrive. Check for supplies and immediate needs. Solicit questions or comments about the previous session and/or share new information and findings. Begin promptly.

Opening Scripture

Luke 16:19–31

Ask a volunteer to light the candle and read aloud. Why did the rich man ignore Lazarus? What might he have done for Lazarus while he was alive? Remind participants there are different forms of poverty (both spiritual and physical). Before beginning your discussion of the lesson handout, ask participants to think about **who might be a "Lazarus" in their own lives or if there has ever been a time when they felt like a "Lazarus."**

> The Church makes a moral judgment about economic and social matters, "when the fundamental rights of the person or the salvation of souls requires it." *CCC 2420*

Journey of Faith

In Short:

- Catholic social justice has its foundation in the Church.
- There are seven themes of Catholic social teaching.
- Christians should always advocate for the poor and vulnerable.

Social Justice

Malala Yousafzai shared the Nobel Peace Prize in 2014, making her the youngest recipient at age 17. Malala came from a Pakistani family that valued education for both boys and girls. Malala was an outspoken advocate for education for all, especially girls who had not always been given that opportunity. When Malala was 15, her advocacy enraged the Taliban regime. Assassins tried to kill her, shooting her in the head. The bullet went through the left side of her forehead, and though it caused serious injuries Malala survived. She vowed to continue her struggle to make education an opportunity available to young people all over the world.

- What can you learn from Malala's story?
- What does it say about acting on your beliefs?

From the beginning, the Church has sought to understand and live out Jesus' command to "love one another as I love you" (John 15:12). The Church isn't just an institution for saving souls but one that cares about the whole person. In addition to spiritual support and nourishment, the Church is called to provide food, shelter, security, respect, and support for the human rights of every person. This is called social responsibility.

> "The duty of making oneself a neighbor to others and actively serving them becomes even more urgent when it involves the disadvantaged, in whatever area this may be."
>
> *CCC 1932*

All Catholic social teaching grows out of the conviction that each one of us has priceless value because we have been created in God's image. We are the summit of all creation, destined to spend eternity with God. No matter how poor, how weak, how sick, or how powerless a person is, she or he is still a child of God.

> "God created mankind in his image; in the image of God he created them; male and female he created them."
>
> *Genesis 1:27*

CCC 1928–1942

Social Justice

- Ask participants to respond to Malala's story. Did her age surprise anyone? How does her story relate to the consistent life ethic or dignity of life?

Why Do We Need Social Justice?

- Discuss why even good people might turn away from or not see the poor and abandoned around them.

Suggested responses include: It might be uncomfortable for us to see, we might think we can't do anything about their situation so we avoid seeing it, and so on.

- Ask participants if they can share examples of when they've seen this happen. These can be examples from their own lives or from the news.

Why Do We Need Social Justice?

Social injustice has existed as long as people have existed, and wise and just men and women have always condemned it. During the time of the great prophets, even the land of Israel was full of injustice and oppression. The words of the great prophets often became a strong warning against injustice.

"When you spread out your hands, I will close my eyes to you; Though you pray the more, I will not listen. Your hands are full of blood! Wash yourselves clean! Put away your misdeeds from before my eyes; cease doing evil; learn to do good. Make justice your aim: redress the wronged, hear the orphan's plea, defend the widow. Come now, let us set things right, says the LORD."

Isaiah 1:15–18

And who were these people whose hands were full of blood? They weren't terrible criminals, but the elders of the people. In Isaiah's time, these were religiously observant people and leaders of the community, but they seemed unaware of the terrible suffering of the poor who surrounded them.

Isaiah proclaims with certainty that we cannot serve the Lord and ignore the poor in our midst. No matter how much we pray, no matter how much time we spend in church, we cannot truly know God if we don't serve our neighbor in need.

When we speak of "the poor," we don't just mean people with no money. "The poor" also refers to those suffering from loneliness, great sadness, or failing mental or physical health. "The poor" includes the elderly woman who lives alone next door, the child in class who can't seem to learn, and the kid on the team who is always on the bench alone. All of us have been in some kind of need.

- What might cause good people to overlook the poor around them?
- How has someone come to your aid in a time of need?

Jesus and Social Justice

Jesus took a stand on social justice from the very beginning of his public life. In the synagogue in Nazareth, he read: "The Spirit of the Lord is upon me, because he has anointed me to bring glad tidings to the poor. He has sent me to proclaim liberty to captives and recovery of sight to the blind, to let the oppressed go free, and to proclaim a year acceptable to the Lord" (Luke 4:18–19; see Isaiah 61:1–2).

The Jesus we see in Scripture is very much involved in the pain and sadness of real life. In Luke's Gospel (16:19–25), Jesus tells the story of Lazarus, a poor man who was "covered with sores," who longed to eat "the scraps that fell from the rich man's table."

When Lazarus died, he was "carried away by angels to the bosom of Abraham." When the rich man died and begged for mercy, Abraham responded, "My child, remember that you received what was good during your lifetime while Lazarus likewise received what was bad; but now he is comforted here, whereas you are tormented" (Luke 16:19–25).

In this story, Jesus isn't condemning the rich man because he was rich. The rich man's sin is that he did nothing. The rich man closed his eyes to the suffering surrounding him. Jesus sends us a powerful message in this story. We are called to actively help the vulnerable, the poor, and the forgotten.

Jesus also tells his followers to take a stand against those who abuse authority or those who profit on others' misery. Jesus said to stand firm, even if that meant getting persecuted, too.

"Before all this happens, however, they will seize and persecute you, they will hand you over to the synagogues and to prisons, and they will have you led before kings and governors because of my name."

Luke 21:12

Jesus' words apply to our lives today, too. When you reach out to the classmate who is ridiculed and ignored, you may be ridiculed and ignored yourself.

Jesus and Social Justice

- Ask participants to think back to the story of Lazarus from the opening Scripture.

- Why does Jesus condemn the rich man for not doing anything?

Suggested responses include: He shut his eyes to Lazarus' suffering, he didn't live his call to treat others like Jesus would, he ignored Lazarus' human dignity, and so on.

- Ask participants if they think Jesus' condemnation of the rich man was just or not in light of Jesus' teachings on social justice. If it's helpful, reread Luke 19–31 as you discuss.

- Ask participants why we should still do the right thing even if it means we could be persecuted. You may also want to bring in examples of saints or holy people who have done the right thing even though it wasn't popular. Or you can use modern examples like Catholics who protest abortion even though it's an unpopular opinion they are sometimes ridiculed for.

- As you review the seven themes of social justice, pause after each one and ask participants to name a way (or ways) this relates to their lives directly or the lives of those around them.

When you take time to visit the elderly woman next door, you will likely lose out on time spent with friends. But when following Jesus gets difficult, we have the Lord's promise: "What eye has not seen, and ear has not heard, and what has not entered the human heart, what God has prepared for those who love him" (1 Corinthians 2:9).

Seven Themes of Social Justice

1. Human life is sacred and every person has dignity.

2. We are called to participate in community and family.

3. All people have rights and responsibilities.

4. We must remember the poor and vulnerable.

5. All work should have dignity and all workers respected.

6. We are one human family, in solidarity.

7. We must care for God's creation.

What Does the Church Teach?

The way we think about Catholic social teaching today began with an 1891 encyclical from Pope Leo XIII called On Capital and Labor (Rerum Novarum). Pope Leo pleaded for an end to the exploitation of working people, called for a just and living wage, and for the right of workers to organize themselves into unions. Pope Leo also made it clear that Catholic tradition supported the right to private property and to fair profit.

The Dogmatic Constitution of the Church (Lumen Gentium), a 1964 document from Vatican II, addressed social issues. It emphasizes what Pope Leo stated: All people should be allowed to work, work should be dignified, and workers should be treated with respect. People who have more than they need should share with those who don't have enough.

From the moment we're born, we rely on others to help us. First, we rely on our parents and family to take care of us. Then we turn to friends to support us, teachers to instruct us, bosses to treat us fairly, neighbors to respect us, the Church to guide us, and the list could go on and on. We have the right to help, support, and compassion as well as the responsibility to provide that help, support, and compassion to others whenever we're able.

- *Where could you apply these teachings to your own life?*

Further Reading on Social Justice

On Capital and Labor (Rerum Novarum) —Pope Leo XIII, 1891

On Christianity and Social Progress (Mater et Magistra)—Pope St. John XXIII, 1961

On Establishing Universal Peace in Truth, Justice, Charity, and Liberty (Pacem in Terris) —Pope St. John XXIII, 1963

Declaration on Religious Freedom (Dignitatis Humanae)—Second Vatican Council, 1965

On the Development of Peoples (Populorum Progressio)—Blessed Pope Paul VI, 1967

On Human Work (Laborem Exercens) —Pope St. John Paul II, 1981

On Social Concern (Sollicitudo Rei Socialis) —Pope St. John Paul II, 1987

The Church and Racism: Toward a More Fraternal Society—Pontifical Council for Justice and Peace, 1989

Compendium of the Social Doctrine of the Church— Pontifical Council for Justice and Peace, 2004

What Does the Church Teach?

- For participants who are interested in a more in-depth understanding of the Church teaching on social justice, refer them to the list of "further reading" in the handout or give them a list of your own. Let them know these lists aren't comprehensive, as there are *many* good Catholic resources on social-justice topics.

But What Can I Do?

- As you finish the lesson, ask participants how they can apply Church teaching to their own lives in addition to the ways listed in the lesson.

With your class, think about your community. Who are the poor in your midst? Brainstorm ways you can give back to your community. Try to come up with at least one action for each of the seven themes of social justice.

Suggested responses include:

1. *We can participate in pro-life events or prayer services, we can actively treat everyone we meet with respect and dignity.*

2. *We can join a volunteer organization or service project that helps our community; we can take on extra chores at home.*

3. *We can think before we act, making sure we're making the moral choice and not just the easy choice.*

4. *We can participate in fund-raisers or collections for the poor, volunteer with an organization that helps the poor and abandoned.*

5. *We can do our work, school assignments, and chores to the best of our abilities without being asked.*

6. *We can make an effort to get to know individuals, not make assumptions based on appearance, ethnicity, religion, and so on.*

7. *We can spend time outside enjoying nature, recycle, make small choices that save energy, like turning out lights when we leave a room.*

CATECHUMENATE

JOURNEY OF FAITH

But What Can I Do?

Share Your Stuff. Jesus asks us to share what we have with those who have less. If you have old clothes, games, electronics, or anything else that you've just outgrown or don't use, consider passing it on.

Share Your Money. This can be a real sacrifice, especially when it feels like you never have enough money yourself. But you don't have to donate millions to make a difference. Try giving up soda, coffee, or other treat once a week and save up that money to donate at the end of the month.

Share Your Time. Life gets busy, and giving away your time can seem more difficult than giving away your money or stuff. But try. Plan one or two hours every week where you give your time to someone else who needs your help, such as tutoring a fellow student in a subject that you know well.

Share Yourself. Being a Christian is all about giving yourself to others. Stand up for the kid who's usually singled out. Ask if you can help when someone seems overwhelmed. Be proud to be a servant.

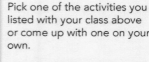

With your class, think about your community.

Who are the poor in your midst? Brainstorm ways you can give back to your community. Try to come up with at least one action for each of the seven themes of social justice.

Pick one of the activities you listed with your class above or come up with one on your own.

Write a plan for how you can put this plan into action. If it's possible, try to carry it out in the next few weeks.

Journey of Faith for Teens: Catechumenate. C16 (826290)
Imprimi Potest: Stephen T. Rehrauer, CSsR, Provincial, Denver Province, the Redemptorists.
Imprimatur: "In accordance with CIC 827, permission to publish has been granted on March 23, 2016, by the Most Reverend Edward M. Rice, Auxiliary Bishop, Archdiocese of St. Louis. Permission to publish is an indication that nothing contrary to Church teaching is contained in this work. It does not imply any endorsement of the opinions expressed in the publication; nor is any liability assumed by this permission."
Journey of Faith © 2000, 2016 Liguori Publications, Liguori, MO 63057. To order, visit Liguori.org or call 800-325-9521. Liguori Publications, a nonprofit corporation, is an apostolate of the Redemptorists. To learn more about the Redemptorists, visit Redemptorists.com. All rights reserved. No part of this publication may be reproduced, distributed, stored, transmitted, or posted in any form by any means without prior written permission. Text: Adapted from *Journey of Faith* © 2000 Liguori Publications. Editors of 2016 *Journey of Faith:* Theresa Nienaber and Pat Fosarelli, MD, DMin. Design: Lorena Mitre Jimenez. Images: Shutterstock. Unless noted, Scripture texts in this work are taken from *New American Bible*, revised edition © 2010, 1991, 1986, 1970 Confraternity of Christian Doctrine, Washington, D.C., and are used by permission of the copyright owner. All Rights Reserved. No part of *New American Bible* may be reproduced in any form without permission in writing from the copyright owner. Excerpts from English translation of the *Catechism of the Catholic Church* for the United States of America © 1994 United States Catholic Conference, Inc. —Libreria Editrice Vaticana; English translation of the *Catechism of the Catholic Church: Modifications from the Editio Typica* © 1997 United States Catholic Conference, Inc. —Libreria Editrice Vaticana. Excerpts from Vatican documents © 2016 Libreria Editrice Vaticana and are used with permission. Compliant with *The Roman Missal, Third Edition.*
Printed in the United States of America. 20 19 18 17 16 / 5 4 3 2 1. Third Edition.

Liguori
PUBLICATIONS
A Redemptorist Ministry

Journaling

Pick one of the activities you listed with your class above or come up with one on your own. Write a plan for how you can put this idea into action. If possible, in the next few weeks try to carry it out.

Closing Prayer

Read Matthew 25:31–40, in which Jesus tells us that when we show care and concern for even the least of our brothers and sisters, we show love and concern for him. Ask for any special intentions after the reading.

Take-home

Sometimes it's easier to look away or not see the poor around us. For the next week, ask participants to make an extra effort to really see the people around them by making eye contact and saying "hi" as they walk past someone or by asking, "Do you need any help?" when they can.

Journey of Faith for Teens
Catechumenate Glossary (alphabetical)

abortion: The intentional and deliberate destruction of a human fetus at any stage after conception. Abortion is an intrinsic evil both from the view of divine revelation and natural law ethics. The right to life is considered the most basic of all human rights, and the right to life of the unborn and innocent is inviolable.

absolution: In the sacrament of penance, this is the form, or words, spoken by the priest for the forgiveness of sins. Through the sign of absolution, God pardons the sinner who, in confession, has shared remorse for his or her sins and the desire to do better to the church's minister, which completes the sacrament of penance.

candidate: Someone who wishes to come into full communion with the Catholic Church and has already been baptized and committed to Jesus Christ. A candidate may be received into the Church at the Easter Vigil or at another Sunday during the year depending on the circumstances surrounding and readiness of the candidate.

capital punishment: The decision of the state to put to death a person proven guilty of one or more serious crimes. The Church states that the death penalty should be carried out only in cases of absolute necessity; when it is impossible to protect society through any other means. As the organization of a penal system improves, cases where capital punishment is the only option become more rare, if not "practically non-existent" (*Evangelium Vitae*, 56).

celibacy: In general, the unmarried state of life. Celibacy is a vocation in which one freely chooses to be unmarried "for the sake of the kingdom of heaven" (Matthew 19:12). This vocation may be lived in a lay state or in a religious institute. Celibacy is required of candidates for the priesthood, with the exception of married men ordained in another Christian tradition.

chrism: Also called the oil of chrism, is used during the sacraments of baptism, confirmation, and during the ordination of a priest or bishop.

commandments (of God): In this context, the commandments refer to the Ten Commandments given by God to Moses on Mount Sinai and interpreted by Jesus Christ.

commission: To be commissioned by God means that we have been sealed, or anointed, by the Spirit as belonging totally to Christ, and are enrolled in service to God forever.

conscience: "Present at the heart of the person, enjoins him at the appropriate moment to do good and to avoid evil. It also judges particular choices, approving those that are good and denouncing those that are evil…. It is a judgment of reason whereby the human person recognizes the moral quality of a concrete act that he is going to perform, is in the process of performing, or has already completed….It is by the judgment of his conscience that man perceives and recognizes the prescriptions of the divine law" (*CCC* 1777–1778).

consistent life ethic: First articulated by Joseph Cardinal Bernardin in a December 6, 1983, lecture at Fordham University, this is the belief that all human life is sacred and that all humans have dignity and our actions should reflect this. A consistent life ethic requires two things. First, that every threat to the dignity of human life is treated. Second, that each threat is given proper weight, recognizing that some involve intrinsically evil acts (such as abortion and euthanasia), while others involve morally problematic acts (such as unjust war and capital punishment).

covenant: This describes a special binding contract between God and the Chosen People. In the covenant of the Old Testament, God promised to be faithful to the people, and they promised to be faithful to God, to worship no other god, and to keep the commandments. The covenant of the New Testament brings the Old Testament covenant to fulfillment in Jesus Christ.

denomination: A branch of Christianity with its own rules of governance and bodies of authority. Many of these branches split from the Catholic Church.

economy: The distribution, production, and consumption of goods in a given geographical location.

elect: The name given to catechumens who have gone through the rite of election and who are preparing to celebrate baptism, confirmation, and the Eucharist at the next Easter Vigil.

euthanasia: "An action or an omission which of itself and by intention causes death, in order that all suffering may in this way be eliminated" *(Declaration on Euthanasia)*. This act is considered morally wrong in all cases, even when the patient may request it, as it is a crime against life and the dignity of the human person. Euthanasia should not be confused with the refusal of extraordinary means of care, which a patient may refuse in conscience. For a more precise differentiation between these two, see *Evangelium Vitae*.

examination of conscience: A prayerful reflection over one's words and deeds using the Gospel and commandments as a guide, to determine where one has sinned against God. The examination of conscience is usually said prior to the sacrament of penance.

free will: From creation, man has been "capable of directing himself toward his true good" *(CCC 1704)*. However, man is also capable of succumbing to the temptation to sin. Free will is our ability to choose what is a true good and to avoid what is evil as well as our ability to discern what is the will of God and what is not.

heresy: The deliberate and obstinate denial by a baptized person of any truth that must be believed as a matter of divine and Catholic faith. Cases of formal heresy, when a baptized person knowingly rejects and denies these truths, are considered a grave sin and result in excommunication. In cases of material heresy, where a baptized person accepts heretical doctrine in good faith and does not knowing reject the truth of the Church, there is no sin or excommunication because they are in good faith.

intrinsic moral evils: Actions that must always be opposed and avoided because they are so deeply flawed they are always opposed to the authentic good of God's creation. An example of an intrinsic moral evil is abortion, which is the intentional taking of an innocent life, an action which can never be aligned with God's plan for creation.

martyr: One who voluntarily suffers death for his or her faith or in defense of some virtue. The Church holds all martyrs in high esteem and honors their memory. Many saints have become saints through their martyrdom.

missionary: One who goes out to spread the good news of Jesus' death and resurrection, and of his presence in the Church to those who would not otherwise hear it. Traditionally missionaries traveled to foreign countries, but anyone who actively evangelizes the good news of Jesus and his Church can be considered a missionary. In fact, the Church's very nature is missionary.

morally problematic: Unlike an intrinsic moral evil, a morally problematic action may, in certain very specific circumstances, be morally licit and so cannot be considered wrong in all circumstances. As with all choices, the object, intention, and circumstances must be taken into consideration to determine the morality of the act (see *CCC 1749–1756*). For the action to be considered morally upright, the object, intention, and circumstances must all be good or, at least, morally neutral.

neophyte: In the context of the RCIA, one who has been "newly planted" in the faith through the sacrament of baptism; a newly baptized Catholic Christian.

penance: Given before the prayer of absolution during the sacrament of penance and reconciliation, this is an act through which the penitent shows remorse for his or her sins and attempts to right any wrongs they've committed and mend any damage to their relationships with others and God.

Pentecost: A liturgical solemnity celebrated fifty days after Easter to commemorate the descent of the Holy Spirit on the apostles and the baptism of an estimated 3,000 new Christians (Acts 2:1–41). It recognizes and celebrates the missionary nature of the Church through the Holy Spirit.

prejudice: A preconceived notion of someone or some group of people that is commonly based on stereotypes rather than actual experience.

presbyters: An "elder" or priest, the presbyterate is the second of the three degrees of the sacrament of Holy Orders. Presbyters assist their bishops in priestly service to the people of God (see *CCC 1567*).

presentation of the Creed: Generally celebrated in the week following the first scrutiny (although it can be celebrated before Lent), this marks the catechumen's acceptance and belief of everything the Creed states. At the time of the presentation of the Creed, the catechumen should be familiar with and understand each of the beliefs cited, which is why this process usually takes late in the catechumenate or during the period of purification and enlightenment.

presentation of the Lord's Prayer: This occurs after the presentation of the Creed and is another important step for the catechumen. The Lord's Prayer is presented because it "fills [the catechumen] with a deeper realization of the new spirit of adoption by which they will call God their Father, especially in the midst of the eucharistic assembly" (*RCIA* 147).

reconciliation: The act of reestablishing a damaged or destroyed relationship. Through his death and resurrection, Jesus reconciled humankind to God after original sin. One can be reconciled to God and with the Church after an act of grave sin through the sacrament of penance.

rite of acceptance: The rite through which an inquirer becomes a catechumen. During this rite, the inquirer states his or her intention to become a baptized member of the Catholic Church amidst the parish community. The community then affirms the inquirer's desire, and the inquirer officially becomes a catechumen.

rite of election: A candidate or catechumen is accepted to receive the sacraments of initiation or their decision to choose the Catholic Church is accepted.

rite of welcoming: Those inquirers who have been previously baptized but who have not received any other sacraments, become candidates in the RCIA process through this rite.

sacrament: A sign and instrument by which the Holy Spirit spreads the grace of Christ throughout the Church, his body. There are seven sacraments celebrated by the Church: baptism, penance and reconciliation, the Eucharist, confirmation, holy orders, marriage, and anointing of the sick.

sacrifice: In the Old Testament, a form of communication and communion with God. These sacrifices usually took the form of a burnt offering or sin offerings. In the New Testament, Christ takes the place of these offerings and becomes the perfect sacrifice which is re-presented in the Eucharist.

scrutinies: Three additional rites during the third, fourth, and fifth Sundays of Lent for the unbaptized elect. The purpose of these scrutinies is to examine one's life, and to reflect on personal sin through the light of God's mercy and grace.

sponsor: It is the sponsor's role to offer support and encouragement during the RCIA process, and then to present the candidate when it is time for them to receive the sacraments. The requirements for a sponsor are the same as for a godparent.

transubstantiation: The word used to describe the change of the whole substance of bread and wine into the whole substance of the Body and Blood of Christ in the Eucharist. Through this change in substance, only the appearance of bread and wine (taste, smell, physical appearance) remain.

witness: The act of a believer living out his or her faith in Jesus Christ, the gospel, and his Church through his or her thoughts, words, and deeds even when those actions result in personal sacrifice or the hostility of others.